German
electoral politics

MANCHESTER
1824

Manchester University Press

ISSUES IN GERMAN POLITICS
Edited by
Professor Charlie Jeffery, Institute for German Studies,
University of Birmingham
Dr Charles Lees, University of Sheffield

Issues in German Politics is a major series on contemporary
Germany. Focusing on the post-unity era, it presents concise,
scholarly analyses of the forces driving change in domestic politics
and foreign policy. Key themes will be the continuing
legacies of German unification and controversies surrounding
Germany's role and power in Europe. The series includes contributions
from political science, international relations and political economy.

Already published:

Annesley: *Postindustrial Germany:*
Services, technological transformation and knowledge in unified Germany

Bulmer, Jeffery and Paterson: *Germany's European diplomacy:*
Shaping the regional milieu

Green: *The politics of exclusion:*
Institutions and immigration policy in contemporary Germany

Gunlicks: *The* Länder *and German federalism*

Harding and Paterson (eds): *The future of the German economy:*
An end to the miracle?

Harnisch and Maull: *Germany as a Civilian Power?*
The foreign policy of the Berlin Republic

Hyde-Price: *Germany and European order:*
Enlarging NATO and the EU

Lees: *The Red–Green coalition in Germany:*
Politics, personalities and power

Longhurst: *Germany and the use of force:*
The evolution of German security policy, 1990–2003

Rittberger (ed.): *German foreign policy since unification: Theories and case studies*

Sperling (ed.): *Germany at fifty-five: Berlin ist nicht Bonn?*

Zaborowski: *Germany, Poland and Europe:*
Conflict, co-operation and Europeanisation

German
electoral politics

Geoffrey K. Roberts

Manchester University Press
Manchester and New York

Distributed exclusively in the USA by Palgrave

Published by Manchester University Press
Oxford Road, Manchester M13 9NR, UK
and Room 400, 175 Fifth Avenue, New York, NY 10010, USA
www.manchesteruniversitypress.co.uk

Distributed exclusively in the USA by
Palgrave, 175 Fifth Avenue, New York,
NY 10010, USA

Distributed exclusively in Canada by
UBC Press, University of British Columbia, 2029 West Mall,
Vancouver, BC, Canada V6T 1Z2

British Library Cataloguing-in-Publication Data
A catalogue record for this book is available from the British Library

Library of Congress Cataloging-in-Publication Data applied for

ISBN 0 7190 6990 4 *hardback*
EAN 978 0 7190 6990 1

First published 2006

15 14 13 12 11 10 09 08 07 06   10 9 8 7 6 5 4 3 2 1

121443

Typeset in Minion
by Servis Filmsetting Ltd, Manchester
Printed in Great Britain
by Biddles Ltd, King's Lynn

Contents

Preface	*page* vii
Abbreviations	ix
Glossary	xi
1	Elections, parties and the political system	1
2	The German electoral system	11
3	Political parties and electoral politics	27
4	The public and electoral politics	50
5	Election campaigns, 1949–2002	73
6	Second-order elections	98
7	Conclusion	118
	Appendices	128
	Bibliography	143
	Index	154

Preface

My debts of gratitude to persons and institutions for their assistance and encouragement relating to my research into German elections are numerous, and extend over a period of more than thirty-five years, since my first study visit to an election campaign in Germany with the late Frank Carter in 1969. Since then, I have been privileged to observe every Bundestag election campaign with the exceptions of 1972 and 1976, and to undertake research relating to parties and elections in Germany on many other occasions. So I must thank the Nuffield Foundation (and most particularly for a grant in 1998 to undertake research into the history and operation of the federal and Länder electoral systems in Germany), the DAAD, the Anglo-German Foundation and the University of Manchester for research grants over those years. Among the many universities and research institutes which have provided facilities the Universities of Mannheim and Chemnitz, the Zentralarchiv at the University of Cologne, the Theodor Heuss Akademie (Gummersbach), the Federal Statistical Office (Wiesbaden) and Forschungsgruppe Wahlen (Mannheim) have been the most frequently used, and their staff have always been generous with their assistance and hospitality. The late Professor Rudolf Wildenmann and Professor Eckhard Jesse have been friends and mentors over many years. Materials supplied by Internationes and the Bundeszentrale für politische Bildung have been of great benefit since the commencement of my research into German elections. Following this very selective listing of my many debts of gratitude, I must acknowledge also the readiness of the various political party offices in Germany and the party research foundations to provide information. The congenial support and assistance of colleagues in the Association for the Study of German Politics have been a great source of encouragement. Elizabeth Carter, Joanna McKay and Thomas Poguntke read some chapters in draft and made valuable suggestions for improvements, and Patricia Hogwood offered useful advice on the structure of the book, to all of whom I am very grateful.

Readers should note that all translations from German sources are my own. All sources cited in the text are listed in the bibliography, with the exception of newspapers and magazines, where details are provided in the source reference in the text. Because many readers will not wish to use sources in German, the bibliography is divided into those published in German and those published in English.

Geoffrey K. Roberts

Abbreviations

ARD	Arbeitsgemeinschaft der öffentlich-rechtlichen Rundfunksanstalten der Bundesrepublik Deutschland (first TV channel)
B '90	Bündnis '90 (Alliance '90: the citizen movement alliance in the GDR)
BfB	Bund freier Bürger (Association of Free Citizens)
CDU	Christlich-Demokratische Union Deutschlands (Christian Democratic Union of Germany)
CSU	Christlich-Soziale Union (Christian Social Union)
DKP	Deutsche Kommunistische Partei (German Communist Party)
DP	Deutsche Partei (German Party)
DSU	Deutsch-Soziale Union (German Social Union)
DVU	Deutsche Volksunion (German People's Union)
EC	European Community
EP	European Parliament
EU	European Union
FDP	Freie Demokratische Partei (Free Democratic Party)
FRG	Federal Republic of Germany
FU	Peace Union
GB/BHE	Gesamtdeutscher Bloc/Bund der Heimatvertriebenen und Entrechteten (All-German Bloc/Association of Expellees and Those Deprived of Rights) – the Refugees Party
GDR	German Democratic Republic
Greens	The Greens (official short name for the party: Alliance '90 – the Greens)
KPD	Kommunistische Partei Deutschlands (Communist Party of Germany)

LDPD	Liberal-Demokratische Partei Deutschlands (GDR Liberal party)
MdB	Mitglied des Bundestages (Member of the Bundestag)
MdL	Mitglied des Landtages (Member of a Landtag)
NPD	Nationaldemokratische Partei Deutschlands (National Democratic Party of Germany)
PDS	Partei des demokratischen Sozialismus (Party of Democratic Socialism)
SED	Sozialistische Einheitspartei Deutschlands (Socialist Unity Party of Germany – GDR party)
SPD	Sozialdemokratische Partei Deutschlands (Social Democratic Party of Germany
SRP	Sozialistische Reichspartei (Socialist Reich Party)
USSR	Former Soviet Union
Z	Zentrum (Centre Party)
ZDF	Zweites Deutsches Fernsehen (second TV channel)

Glossary

Basic Law	The constitution of the FRG adopted in 1949
Bizone	The name given to the linked British and American occupation zones in West Germany which came into effect in 1947
Bundesrat	The upper chamber of the federal legislature, representing the Länder
Bundestag	The popularly elected lower chamber of the federal legislature
Bundesverfassungsgericht	Federal Constitutional Court
Bundesversammlung	The electoral college which chooses the federal president
Bundeswahlleiter	Electoral Commissioner
Democratic Awakening	Demokratischer Aufbruch: a party connected to the citizens' movement formed in the GDR in 1989, embracing political and social reform
eastern Germany	The former territory of the GDR, comprising the five 'new' Länder, together with Berlin
EMNID	An opinion survey research institute
5 per cent clause	The clause in the Electoral Law which requires parties which have not won at least three constituency seats to obtain 5 per cent of party list votes in an election in order to be allocated a proportional distribution of seats
Fraktion (pl.: Fraktionen)	An officially recognised parliamentary

	party group in the Bundestag or other legislature in Germany; in the Bundestag, a party needs 5 per cent of MdBs in order to obtain Fraktion status
Gemeinde	Local government district
Gesamtstimme	Aggregate of constituency and list votes
'grand coalition'	A coalition of the two largest parties, the CDU–CSU and the SPD; the federal coalition in 1966–69 was a 'grand coalition'
Infas	An opinion survey research institute (Institut für angewandte Sozialwissenschaft)
Land (pl.: Länder)	The states which together constitute the FRG
Landkreise	A local government area equivalent to an English county
Landtag	A parliament of a Land
Nazis	The National Socialist Party, led by Hitler, which ruled Germany during the Third Reich, 1933–45
'new' Länder	The five Länder created in 1990 in the former territory of the GDR when Germany was reunified; these Länder had existed in the GDR prior to their abolition in 1952
Regierungsbezirke	Land administrative regions
Reichstag	The German lower chamber of the legislature in the Second Empire (1870–1918) and Weimar Republic (1919–33), and the name of the building where the Bundestag now assembles since its transfer from Bonn to Berlin
Schill party	Officially titled *Partei der rechtsstaatlichen Offensive* (Party for the Promotion of the Rule of Law), which won seats in the Hamburg 2001 Land election under its founder and leader, Schill
Stadtkreise	A local government district in a city
STATT Party	A new party ('STATT' means 'instead of . . .'), which won seats in the Hamburg Land election in 1993

'Superwahljahr'	'Super-election year', the term applied to 1994 when the Bundestag election took place in the same year as several Land and local government elections, as well as the EP election and the election of the federal president
Überhangmandate	'Surplus seats': seats additional to the normal number of seats in the Bundestag, won by a party because it receives more seats in constituencies in a Land than it is entitled to on the basis of its share of party list votes in that Land
Volkskammer	The parliament of the GDR
Volkspartei	A 'people's party', intended to appeal to all sections of the electorate
Wende	A change of political direction. The term was applied to the policy programme of the Kohl government when it replaced the SPD–FDP coalition in 1982, and to the downfall of the Communist regime in the GDR and the reunification of Germany which then followed (1989–90)

1
Elections, parties and the political system

There are many ways of analysing German politics. Recent studies have, for example, focused on policymaking, on institutions (Helms 2000), and on the interface between German politics and the politics of the European Union (Bulmer, Jeffery and Paterson 2000; Sturm and Pehle 2001). All these approaches are valid, but none captures all the intricate interconnections and multiple dimensions of the political process in Germany. The once-popular focus on electoral politics has been neglected of late, yet it can be asserted that electoral politics is one of the most pervasive elements of the German political process, indeed the bedrock upon which the political system is supported. It is also still an important approach – if not always in the ways in which it is important in other European democracies such as the United Kingdom or France. In this book, the case is made for retaining some degree of concentration on electoral politics in order to understand and appreciate the German political system and political process.

The starting-point has to be the electoral system. The behaviour, strategies and decisions of the electorate, of party politicians at federal and Land levels and of the campaign advisers who now possess an increasingly prominent role now in all the principal parties at every election, are shaped and constrained by the electoral system. The existence of a 5 per cent requirement for proportional allocation of seats in the Bundestag and in Land parliaments, and the option of split voting, are just two obvious examples of this fact. Chapter 2 therefore reviews the development of the present-day electoral system, the few serious attempts that have been made to change the fundamental attributes of the system and the importance in recent Bundestag elections of previously neglected details (concerning surplus seats, for instance). The chapters 3–5 examine the ways in which parties on the one hand, and the electorate on the other, react to the electoral process, as 'producers' and 'consumers', as it were. Chapter 5 consists of a brief review of each Bundestag election since 1949, looking at particularly interesting and pertinent features of the campaign, the operation of the electoral system and the outcome of the election. Chapter 6 moves from a focus on Bundestag elections to an analysis of 'second-order' elections (though that description itself requires discussion): the elections to local councils, to the European Parliament (EP) and to Land legislatures. Attention is focused on the inter-relationships between Bundestag elections and these 'second-order' elections, to highlight the important differences in the various electoral systems used (all are varieties of a proportional representation system), and to consider the effects which such elections can have on national politics. The concluding chapter 7 poses the question: does electoral politics matter? It assesses the effectiveness of the German mixed-member electoral system and considers the importance of a system of electoral politics in which only rarely do governments change as an immediate result of Bundestag elections.

The concept of 'electoral politics'

It will be obvious that this book is about more than superficial aspects of electoral campaigns and election results, important though those are. The term 'electoral politics' has been chosen as the title of this book to emphasise the complexity of the inter-play of different aspects of elections and to draw attention to the more extensive ways in which elections affect the political system. Elections, then, in the context of electoral politics, are much more than dramatic interruptions to the normal, day-to-day, business of government. It will be suggested in later chapters that, in some ways, politicians are caught up in a permanent election campaign. What is normally regarded as the 'election campaign' – the period when the posters appear on the hoardings, the politicians and their helpers go in search of votes at election rallies or on the streets and the mass media elevate election news to their headlines – is, in fact, the product of months and years of planning and preparation. However, no claim is made that all politics in Germany is 'electoral politics'. The quasi-diplomacy and multi-level political interactions that mark relations with the institutions of the European Union (EU), the manoeuvrings of administrative politics within the ministries in Berlin and in the Länder capitals, the inter-governmental politics within the federal system, are all obviously important features of German political life, and are not, or are only indirectly, affected by electoral politics. Interest groups are another important, if neglected, set of actors in the political system. The cross-party 'coastal Mafia' of Members of the Bundestag (MdBs) from Bremen, Hamburg, Schleswig-Holstein and Lower Saxony who secure key positions on the budget and finance committees of the Bundestag and are thus in a position to protect projects such as military installations, beneficial to the economies of their northern region, is one example (*Der Spiegel* 3 August 1998: 42–3). The trade unions which protect the high subsidies of coal miners in North Rhine-Westphalia or the job security and pay levels of those working in the construction of automobiles, the associations which look after the interests of pharmacists, dentists, estate agents and other professions, agricultural interest groups and the organisations concerned with the interests of those in the public service are other examples of groups which play often a significant role in politics but which are relatively unaffected by the outcomes of electoral politics.

Clearly, the electoral system sets the parameters for electoral politics. Germany has a parliamentary system of government, not a presidential system. So elections to the national legislature influence – and occasionally, indeed, may determine – which party or combination of parties forms the government. The details of the system – in particular, the two-vote ballot paper, permitting split-voting and the 5 per cent requirement for allocations of list seats – affect the party composition of the Bundestag and the alternative coalitions which may be constructed. For example, a different government would have been in office in 1969 had either the radical right-wing National Democratic Party (NPD) gained representation, or the liberal Free Democratic Party (FDP) lost it, yet their vote shares were only 1.5 per cent apart. Split-voting ensured the continued representation in the Bundestag of the FDP in 1969, 1972, 1983, 1987, 1994 and 1998: all elections in which the party's share of constituency votes fell below 5 per cent, but where list vote-share was above 5 per cent (see chapter 4). With the exception of 1998, the FDP was also able to participate in the coalition government formed after those elections, which it could not have done had only those constituency votes determined the proportional allocation of seats. The anxieties which German and non-German politicians have had about the possible resurgence of right-wing extremism have also focused attention on the 5 per cent requirement in the electoral system. So far, of such extreme right-wing parties, only the NPD has come within 1 per cent of qualifying for Bundestag seats since the 1950s, though in Land and local council elections (as well as in elections to the EP) such parties have been occasionally successful in winning seats.

The political parties

Electoral politics is party politics. So campaigning, electoral behaviour by the individual voters, coalition formation and many other aspects of electoral politics are influenced by the shape and pattern of the party system. Many historians hold the view that the failure of the Weimar Republic was due in great measure to the inability of the party system to integrate voters adequately or to demonstrate sufficient political flexibility to form strong and stable coalition governments. This opinion had important consequences for the establishment of a democratic political system in the western zones of occupation once the Second World War was over.

The post-1945 party system which emerged did so under the strict discipline of the licensing system imposed by the occupying governments in their zones. This meant that parties were, at least formally, democratic in their aims and organisation, and that relatively few parties were granted licences in each zone. Some of the parties which did obtain licences were the re-established organisations of pre-war political parties: the Social Democrats (SPD), the Communist Party (KPD) and the Centre party (Zentrum: Z) were the most important examples. Others, such as the Christian Democrats (CDU and, in Bavaria, the CSU) and the Liberals (the FDP), were newly formed parties intended to replace one or more of the Weimar political parties. For the first Bundestag election a large number of parties competed, and many won seats. However, several factors swiftly reduced the number of successful parties so that in 1961 only three parties remained in the Bundestag, increasing to four in 1983 when the Greens won seats. After reunification five parties had seats from 1990 until the Party of Democratic Socialism (PDS) lost its representation as a party group in the 2002 election (though two PDS MdBs were elected in constituencies). These factors included the operation in 1953 and 1956 of a more restrictive 5 per cent requirement to win list seats, the constitutional ban on two parties in 1952 and 1956, the ability of the CDU to absorb smaller conservative parties and the tendency of the electorate to concentrate their votes on the two largest parties.

Attempts from time to time to establish a successful new party to the right of the CDU have all failed. There are parties of the extreme right, but these have only sporadic electoral success in second-order elections. None has managed to win seats in the Bundestag since the 1950s. The idea in the 1970s of using the CSU as a fourth party, garnering extra votes for a Christian Democrat majority, came to nothing, especially since any extension of the CSU's electoral activities beyond Bavaria would inevitably open the way for the CDU to present candidates in Bavaria, to the chagrin of the CSU. Other right-wing parties which have from time to time sought to benefit from periods of CDU electoral weakness, such as the Bund freier Bürger (Association of Free Citizens) in 1994, the East German Deutsche Sozial-Union (German Social Union) formed in 1990 and the Schill party (2001–2), have all failed to make an electoral breakthrough, apart from a few, transient, successes in Land elections in some cases (Raschke and Tils 2002: 55–7).

Of course, the parties in the Bundestag have undergone changes over the years. They have changed their ideologies, in part because such changes were necessary in order to compete more effectively in elections. The SPD became a more open party when it marked the abandonment of its socialist ideology at the Bad Godesberg Congress in 1959, after which it gained between 2 and 3 per cent of vote-share at every election until 1972, when it became the largest single party for the first time. The Christian Democrats diluted their early statist and welfare-oriented policies, to become more recognisably a conservative party, though one that retained its links to the churches. The FDP underwent a thorough change of direction during its 'wilderness years' in opposition to the 'grand coalition' (1966–69), but then in the early 1980s veered once more to the right of the political spectrum, especially on economic and financial policies. The Greens became a much more pragmatic party after the shock defeat in 1990, when the western German Greens lost representation in the Bundestag. These changes of course affected how the parties regarded each other as potential coalition partners, as well as how the electorate regarded the parties. For example, changes in the CDU and the Greens have meant that discussion concerning the possibility of those parties someday forming governing coalitions at federal or Land level are no longer too fanciful. The materialist–post-materialist cleavage is less prominent. Generational changes in the two parties mean that the CDU is more open to libertarian ideas embraced by some Greens, while the Greens have for their part lessened their demands for policy solutions based on more state intervention and socialist approaches. Both parties would benefit strategically from such an additional coalition option. However, the gap between the parties is still wide. While co-operation in

Table 1 **Party membership: end-of-year data, 1991–2003**

	2003	2000	1991
SPD	650,798	734,693	919,871
CDU	587,244	616,722	751,163
CSU	176,950	181,021	184,513
PDS	65,753	83,475	172,579
FDP	65,192	62,721	137,853
Greens	44,091	46,631	38,873

Sources: Niedermayer (2004); *Das Parlament* (1 March 2002); PDS website.

local government is easier because local politics is more issue-based, the ideological basis of national and Land-level political issues makes such co-operation still a distant prospect (Kleinert 2004: 72–4).

The parties have also undergone changes in their membership. The size of their memberships has fallen in recent years. Though a comparison between 2003 and 1991 is distorted by special factors concerning party membership data in eastern Germany following reunification,[1] the general declining trend for all parties except the Greens (which later benefited from the merger with Alliance '90) can be clearly observed.

These memberships, as in many other countries, were getting older on average. The proportion of members over sixty years of age ranged from 33.4 per cent for the FDP to 45.7 per cent for the CDU (and the PDS in 2002 had 68.7 per cent over sixty years of age).[2] Partly in response to the Green party's insistence on involving females more intensively in politics, the parties have also increased the proportion of their membership which is female. Apart from the PDS, again an outlier with 45.8 per cent female membership (a function to some extent of the age factor), the range of female members is 17.9 per cent for the CSU to 37.1 per cent for the Greens (Niedermayer 2004: 316, 319–20). One way of attracting more female members is to ensure that women become party office-holders and are elected or appointed to public office. The parties have done this by means of formal quotas (the Greens, the SPD and the PDS) and 'targets' (the CDU), as well as by other means (McKay 2004a).

The importance of electoral politics in the German political system

How can the importance of electoral politics in the German political system be substantiated empirically? Three indicators suggest themselves:

the expenditure of political resources by the parties and politicians; the weight given to electoral aspects of the Basic Law by the Constitutional Court in its decisions; and the attention given to electoral politics by the mass media.

The parties and politicians devote considerable resources to preparation for and the conduct of election campaigns. Significant proportions of the budgets of political parties are devoted to election purposes. In return, large amounts of public funds are paid to parties as subsidies, and the amounts vary according to the electoral success of the parties. Beyond these direct measures of financial resources attributed to electoral politics, indirectly resources required for membership recruitment, local and regional activities and the operation of party central offices are all related to the desire to win votes and to win elections. Of course, it is impossible to draw a line between activities concerned with representation of citizens and of interest groups and those designed to improve the chances of an individual or a party winning an election. Is some activity of an MdB in a constituency aimed at helping with a local problem, or with ensuring favourable publicity and the gratitude of a local organisation which will be of benefit to that politician at the next election? The development of policies or the revision of more general party programmes are undertaken by parties because politicians want to affect policy issues: for example, environmental protection; the possible admission of Turkey to the EU; reform of labour market conditions; changes to the system of health insurance. Nevertheless, it is obvious also that certain policies will be more popular than others, that unpopular policies will lose votes and that in particular the image of a party as defined by its basic programme can have a direct effect on voting support. The Bad Godesberg Programme of the SPD in 1959 or the Freiburg Theses of the FDP in 1971, though in both cases confirming rather than creating the adaptation of party identity for those parties, were influential in bringing to the attention of the electorate the fundamental changes which those parties had undergone. So, whether directly or more indirectly, the financial or other resources which parties and politicians devote to electoral politics is a measure of the significance of elections in the political system.

The Constitutional Court, by the various decisions it has made concerning the constitutional aspects of elections and representation, has emphasised the importance of electoral politics (Kommers 1997: 181–99). It has made judgements about the validity of the 5 per cent clause both as applied in Bundestag elections and for elections to Land legislatures, the freedom of parties to alter party lists after an election (held by the Constitutional Court to offend the principle of 'direct elections'), the apportionment of constituencies, the constitutionality of proposals for adaptation of the electoral system to be used in the first Bundestag election following German reunification, the existence of surplus seats and the constitutionality of the three-constituency alternative to the 5 per cent qualification for proportional representation. In doing so, it has generated a set of statements which constitute precedent for future cases, relating to issues such as the purposes of the 5 per cent requirement (including the creation of a legislature which can function free from the complication of having too many small parties), the co-existence of constituency and list election within the electoral system and the role of parties in electoral politics. To the cases directly concerned with the electoral system can be added verdicts about the constitutionality of state payments to political parties, the prohibition of parties (and hence of their ability to present candidates at elections), rules about provision of broadcasting and other facilities (such as meeting halls owned by local councils) to political parties in election campaigns with regard to the equal treatment of parties, and the propriety of government departments publishing advertisements emphasising their achievements close to an election campaign (Kommers 1997: 177–81, 201–29). The attention of the Constitutional Court to the finer details of the electoral system and its surrounding procedures (such as postal voting) and their interpretations of the principles of 'free, equal, secret and direct' election as stated in the Basic Law emphasise the importance of electoral politics in the democratic system of Germany.

The mass media in Germany devote considerable attention to electoral politics (Eilders, Degenhardt, Herrmann and von der Lippe 2004). The press and broadcasting agencies, in their variety of forms from the populist *Bild Zeitung* to the *Frankfurter Rundschau* and the ZDF TV channel, give prominence to stories about election campaigns and election outcomes, but also at other times they report on issues related to elections, such as potential coalition strategies, choice of chancellor-candidates, factionalism within parties and the possible effects on their election chances, the constraints of electoral politics on policymaking likely adversely to affect certain interests. The close relationship between, on the one hand, certain newspapers, magazines such as *Focus* and *Der Spiegel* and TV channels such as ZDF and, on the other hand, opinion survey institutes such as *Forschungsgruppe Wahlen*, is another indication of the extent to which electoral politics has significance.

The dynamic aspect of German electoral politics

Though significant aspects of German electoral politics treated in these chapters can be stated in terms of trends (such as the rise and decline in electoral turnout, or changes in the number of parties with seats in the Bundestag), it is dangerous to extrapolate too confidently from past data. The propensity of governing parties to underperform in Land elections compared to the trend line between two successive Bundestag elections, identified by Dinkel and discussed in chapter 6, has been shown to be less pronounced in recent years, for example. Politics, and especially electoral politics, occurs in a dynamic situation. Circumstances never repeat themselves exactly; contexts change; political leaders are replaced. Parties learn from past experiences. So there is a dynamic aspect derived simply from the passage of time. Despite the seeming stability of governing coalitions in Germany, for instance, the partners when a coalition is first formed have a different relationship than when that coalition is eight years old, facing another Bundestag election and the parties have developed a more trusting or a more wary relationship with each other. The electoral system itself comes into the equation in unforeseen ways: who would have imagined in the 1987 election that either the number of surplus seats would increase several-fold and come near in 1994 to creating an otherwise non-existent chancellor majority, or that in 1994 the 'three-seat' alternative to the 5 per cent qualification for party list seats would once more prove to be relevant? The case of Germany is special in another way. There is a dynamic element related to German reunification. Two political systems merged, and voters in the two parts of the enlarged German state had very different histories, very different experiences of politics, very different attitudes to electoral politics and to political parties. The changes which have occurred in the party system since 1990 have been partly the result of the continuation of trends observable in the 'old' Federal Republic, partly changes impelled by the fact of German reunification (Saalfeld 2002). The ways in which the western part of the Federal Republic, having experienced over forty years of democratic politics and eleven Bundestag elections, approached the twelfth Bundestag election – and the first for reunified Germany – were very different from the attitudes and hopes of the citizens of eastern Germany, who had experienced only a few months of democratic politics and one democratic election just eight months earlier (together with more recent Länder elections) and who attached very different connotations to the concepts of political parties and party membership. So analysis of any aspect of German electoral politics must incorporate an appreciation of this dual dynamism: the effects of changes produced by trends over time, and the enormous adjustment made by political institutions, politicians and citizens to German reunification. These themes relating to trends and changes will recur throughout the book.

Notes

1 This is because some western German parties 'inherited' large registers of members of eastern German parties with which they had merged in the summer of 1990. For a while, for example, the FDP had a much larger eastern German membership than it had in western Germany. Very soon many of these 'inherited' members failed to renew their subscriptions and numbers declined to more normal levels. By 1994 the CDU had only two-thirds and the FDP only one-third of its eastern German membership of 1990 (Roberts 1997: 128–31).
2 No data on age were available from the Greens.

2

The German electoral system

Do electoral systems matter?

Evidence suggests that electoral systems *do* matter, and that politicians and the public think that they make a difference. There have been many examples of electoral systems which have been changed: some in order to obtain partisan advantage, such as Mitterrand's self-serving experiment with proportional representation for the French National Assembly elections in March 1986. In other cases, reform has been undertaken in order to improve the representation function of the electoral system: the change to an additional member system in 1993 in New Zealand is one example. There have been several other cases of proposals to change the system, which for one reason or another, were not adopted – and the reasons for non-adoption also emphasise the importance of electoral systems (the Federal Republic of Germany in the period of the 'grand coalition'; Ireland in 1959 and 1968; the United Kingdom, most recently following the report of the Jenkins Commission in 1998). Changes to the electoral system do not always produce the outcomes which have been anticipated, though, and experts disagree about the extent to which electoral systems may affect electoral outcomes, party systems or forms of government. Bogdanor goes so far as categorically to contend that 'any theory making the electoral system a fundamental causative factor in the development of party systems cannot be sustained' (Bogdanor 1983: 254).

Nevertheless, since 1948 politicians and political scientists concerned with electoral systems in Germany have generally taken the view that the choice of electoral system matters. It matters in relation to democratic values, and the Basic Law, which does not prescribe any particular form of electoral system, does require such a system to be general, direct, free, equal and secret (Article 38). Within those broad requirements, various electoral systems could be designed, and the work of the committee of the Parliamentary Council in 1948–49 (see below) was directed at selecting a system that not only met those requirements, but also incorporated other desired attributes. The system which they then recommended, and the reformed versions of that system adopted in 1953 and 1956, were not accepted enthusiastically by all the political parties. This was because it was obvious that where one system (or one variation of that system) would benefit certain parties, a different system – at that time – would benefit other parties. Party advantage was also the reason for the proposition in the period of the 'grand coalition' that the electoral system should be changed to one based more closely on simple majority single-member constituencies, as in the United Kingdom, as well as the eventual decision by the SPD that it could not support such a change. Some political scientists have attempted to demonstrate that the proportional representation system utilised in the Weimar Republic made a major contribution to the replacement of the Weimar Republic by the Nazi regime (Hermens 1968).

How can electoral systems make a difference? There are at least three important aspects of electoral systems which can affect the structure of the party system and the power of parties within electoral politics. These are the ease with which small parties can obtain seats (including the effect on electoral behaviour of the proportionality of the electoral system); the exaggerative effects of the electoral system on the majority of the governing party or coalition; and the extent to which party hierarchies can control the composition of its parliamentary party group.

Choice of electoral system, or reform of provisions of an existing electoral system, can for small parties often mean survival in, or elimination from, the legislature. Since 1961 only two parties which had representation in the Bundestag have ever lost it: the Greens in 1990 in West Germany, under a one-off post-reunification variation of the electoral system, and the PDS in 2002, then restricted to two constituency seats only. However, several parties before 1961 lost representation. There are also many examples of parties losing membership in Land parliaments, under similar electoral rules concerning the 5 per cent requirement as apply in a Bundestag election: the FDP and the Greens in several Länder (and especially recently in eastern Länder), the extreme right-wing DVU in Bremen, Saxony-Anhalt and Schleswig-Holstein, the Republicans in Berlin and Baden-Württemberg, the Employment for Bremen party (*Arbeit für Bremen*) in 1999, and the STATT party and Schill party in

Hamburg, for instance. However, the need to obtain 5 per cent of votes to secure proportional representation did not prevent the Greens from entering Land parliaments and the Bundestag in the 1980s. The DVU won seats in the Brandenburg Land parliament in 1999 and 2004, and the NPD won seats in the 2004 Saxony Land election. The Greens and FDP have often regained representation in Land parliaments.

The perceived possible effects of the electoral system on the likelihood of parties winning seats in the legislature influences electoral behaviour. Voters are less likely to support small parties if there seems little chance of them winning seats. The German electoral system offers parties proportional representation, but only if they are sufficiently well supported as to meet the 5 per cent qualification for distribution of list seats – or have sufficient locally concentrated support to win at least three constituency seats instead. So voters have to take a view on the prospects of small parties. This may account for the fact that few parties score in the 2–4 per cent range: either they are seen to have a good chance of election, and sympathisers then support them (perhaps to ensure that they do get over the 5 per cent mark, and thus be available as a coalition partner: see chapter 4), or their chances are seen to be negligible, so voters who otherwise would support them try to avoid wasting their votes, and support another party instead. In 1998 the Republicans (1.8 per cent of list votes) was the highest-scoring party of those obtaining less than 5 per cent. In 2002 only the PDS (4.0 per cent) of unsuccessful parties obtained a vote-share greater than 1 per cent. From 1972 to 1990, all the parties which did not win seats obtained only between 0.5 per cent and 2.1 per cent of list votes in total.

Other aspects of the German electoral system which may influence voting behaviour are the two-vote system, with separate votes for the constituency candidate and the party list, which permits 'split-voting' (see chapter 4) and the possibility in a very few cases of attempting to secure 'surplus seats' for a party by tactical voting (though this is nearly impossible to bring to fruition by intent). Turnout may be influenced by the fact that the system is proportional, and therefore few votes are wasted, unless given to parties with very little hope of winning seats.

The choice of electoral system affects the exaggerative effect of votes on the proportion of seats which a party wins, and hence on the possibility of a party with fewer than half the votes winning over half the seats. In the United Kingdom this occurs regularly: thanks to the disproportionality of the first-past-the-post system, a party with under 40 per cent of votes can easily win well over 50 per cent of seats. The German system has only a small exaggerative effect, resulting from two factors. From time to time so-called 'surplus seats' are created (see below), which benefits one or other of the two largest parties. The exclusion of parties which obtain fewer than 5 per cent of list votes means that parties which do secure proportional representation win a slightly larger share of seats than their vote-share would indicate. Thus in 2002, taking these two factors together, the SPD (38.5 per cent of votes) won 41.6 per cent of seats. The Christian Democrats (also with 38.5 per cent of votes) won 41.1 per cent of seats. The Greens won 9.1 per cent of seats but only 8.6 per cent of the list votes. The FDP won 7.8 per cent of seats but 7.4 per cent of votes. The PDS, on the other hand, having failed to qualify for an allocation of list seats by securing only 4 per cent of list votes, secured only two constituency seats, equivalent to 0.3 per cent of total seats. At every Bundestag election, had the result been decided only on constituency seats won, the governing party would always have had a vastly larger percentage share of seats than its percentage share of list votes.

The German electoral system

Basically the electoral system used in Bundestag elections since 1957 (and amended only in minor detail since then) is simple and straightforward. There are three main features, and two complicating factors.

The three main features are:

- The system is one *of proportional representation*. After the two complicating factors are taken into account, each party will receive a percentage share of Bundestag seats corresponding to its percentage share of list votes (sometimes called 'second' votes).
- *Each voter has two votes*. The first vote is used to elect a constituency candidate by means of a simple majority election in single-member constituencies. The second vote is used to vote for a party list in the Land in which the constituency is located (thus voters in Stuttgart vote for Baden-Württemberg party lists, and voters in Erfurt for Thuringia party lists). 'Split votes' are permitted: the voter can choose a constituency candidate of one party but vote for the Land list of a different party.
- Seats are then allocated to parties in proportion to the total number of valid list votes received. This is calculated on the basis of the total vote for all the Land lists of each party that qualifies for a proportional dis-

tribution of seats (see below). However, the *total seats allocated include any constituency seats* won by the party. So a party entitled to a total of 300 seats, but which has won 160 constituency seats, would obtain 140 list seats in addition. Had the party won only 100 constituency seats, then 200 list seats would have been allocated.

The two complicating factors are:

- Only parties which obtain *at least 5 per cent* of the total votes cast for party lists qualify for any list seats, except for parties which have won at least three constituency seats. A party winning one or two constituency seats retains these (as the PDS did in 2002), but receives no additional seats. One consequence of this is that parties which do obtain a proportional allocation of seats all end up with slightly more than their apparent share: a party with 44 per cent of list votes might obtain 46 per cent of seats, because 4 per cent of list votes were cast for parties which did not qualify for list seat distribution.
- Because any constituency seats won cannot be taken away from a candidate or party, and because calculation of seats awarded to party lists is done on a Land-by-Land basis, it is possible for a party to have won more constituency seats in a Land than its total allocation of seats in that Land. It retains these for the duration of the legislative period, and the total number of MdBs increases temporarily. Such *surplus seats* are additional to the total proportional allocation for that party, so distort proportional representation of parties in the Bundestag (see Appendix 1).

The electoral system is based upon extensive constitutional and statutory provisions. As stated above, the Basic Law (Article 38) contains the requirement that the electoral system provided by legislation be general, direct, free, equal and secret. So the versions of the Electoral Law passed in 1953 and 1956 had to conform to these parameters. The Electoral Law is a detailed set of rules which prescribes not only the methods by which votes are translated into seats, as described above, but also the technical arrangements for scrutiny of voting procedures and counting of votes, the format of the ballot paper, rules to guide decisions concerning spoilt ballot papers, provisions for postal voting and so on. Certain sections of the Party Law also are relevant to elections, such as the decision concerning whether or not an organisation can claim the legal status of a political party, and thus be qualified to nominate candidates in constituencies and offer lists of candidates in a Land.

The whole electoral procedure is under the oversight of the Electoral Commissioner, an officer of the Federal Statistical Office. The Commissioner is appointed for an indefinite term by the Federal Minister of the Interior, and by convention the minister appoints the Director of the Federal Statistical Office. That official examines the bids by organisations to be recognised as parties (even if not all such successful bids result in participation in the election). Each organisation has to submit a form giving its name, any supplementary description it wishes to provide, the names of its executive committee, its official address, its statutes and programme. In 2002, for example, bids were received from, among others, eccentric parties such as the Anarchist Pogo Party (whose aims included support for 'peace, freedom and adventure, as well as the right to be unemployed'), the Party of Non-Voters (who wanted substantial reform of the electoral system, reduction in the size of the Bundestag and more direct democracy) and the Motorists' Party, as well as fringe parties or parties which in the past had been more successful than in their present condition, such as the DKP (German Communist Party), DSU (German Social Union), New Forum and the Centre Party, a party as old as the modern state of Germany itself (Statistisches Bundesamt 2002). Parties which have been prohibited by the Federal Constitutional Court are excluded from the electoral process. So far, only the extreme right-wing Socialist Reich Party (SRP) in 1952 and the Communist Party of Germany (KPD) in 1956 have been banned by the Constitutional Court. An attempt to ban the National Democratic Party (NPD) in 2002 was rejected by the Constitutional Court. According to the Electoral Law (paragraphs 13, 15(2)), individuals may be prohibited from standing as candidates as a result of legal procedures which remove from them the right to vote or to be candidates in public elections, as well as because of mental incapacity.

The evolution of the German electoral system

The current electoral system has developed, with few significant changes, from that designed by the Parliamentary Council in 1949. The design of that system was itself strongly influenced, if negatively, by what many regarded as the undesirable effects of the system used in the Weimar Republic, and, more positively, by systems already in use for Land elections and by the preferences of the Allied occupation governments.

The system used by the Second Empire (1871–1918) for elections to the Reichstag was a two-ballot system in single-member constituencies, very similar to that currently used for elections to the National Assembly in the French Fifth Republic. On the first ballot, those candidates were elected who had secured an absolute majority of votes cast. In constituencies where that did not occur, the two leading candidates entered a second (run-off) ballot. Only males over the age of twenty-five had the right to vote.

The founders of the Weimar Republic, including the SPD who had been disadvantaged by several features of the pre-First World War system (such as unfair design of constituencies), were determined to adopt an electoral system which corresponded to their rather idealistic notions of democratic political structures and procedures. So the system was one of almost unrestricted proportional representation, including female suffrage, based on regional constituencies. Each party list was allocated a seat for every 60,000 votes received. Surplus votes were then aggregated as fractional remainders at a second level, based on groupings of regional constituencies, and again a seat was awarded for every 60,000 votes. Finally, surplus votes at this level were aggregated at the national level and a third allocation of seats was made, though only to party lists which already had obtained seats at the lower levels of allocation. This meant that (a) even small parties could obtain a few seats in the Reichstag; (b) there was little electoral penalty for splitting away from a party to form a new party; and (c) the size of the Reichstag varied with turnout. Certainly the lack of hindrance to small and breakaway parties meant that numerous parties had seats in the Reichstag: in 1932 fifteen parties won seats; of these only seven had five or more representatives in the Reichstag. This large number of parties in turn meant that coalitions tended to consist of several parties, any one of which could bring down the government by withdrawal from the coalition. To this extent, instability of government reinforced the other negative factors which contributed to the downfall of the Republic. It is less clear that the electoral system must be blamed for the success of the Nazis in coming to power.

When the Parliamentary Council met to draft a provisional constitution for the new Bonn Republic, it obviously had to provide an electoral system to elect the first Bundestag (which could then use the normal legislative process to pass an Electoral Law to govern future elections). The British wanted a system which emphasised single-member constituencies with election by simple majority (sometimes called plurality election), as used to elect the House of Commons. The Americans were less concerned with the mode of election, but wanted the federal basis of the state to be recognised in the system adopted. The French were familiar with proportional representation systems, but were wary of adoption by the Federal Republic of a list-based proportional representation system, as this would tend to centralise the power of the parties which, in the circumstances of the time, they distrusted (Lange 1975: 368). The Länder had used a variety of systems of election, though all included some degree of proportional representation, which seemed to be the principle acceptable to most Germans.

A committee of the Parliamentary Council was given the task of recommending a system. Its debates mixed arguments about detail with diagnoses of the extent to which the Weimar electoral system had brought about the disasters which afflicted Germany from 1930 onwards. Parties obviously considered their own electoral advantage, and put pressure on their representatives on the committee to insist on particular aspects which would benefit their party. The Christian Democrats, for example, pressed throughout the discussions for a majoritarian system. The ministers-president, who had played such an important role in summoning the Parliamentary Council under orders from the Allies, served as a mediating institution between the committee of the Parliamentary Council and the occupation authorities when the Allies were unwilling to accept particular proposals from the committee (Lange 1975: 368). In the end, compromises were reached and a system was recommended which would provide proportional representation of parties within each Land (the federal principle), but – at the insistence of the Allies – with a majority of seats (60 per cent) filled by simple majority voting in single-member constituencies and the remaining 40 per cent elected from party lists to secure proportionality. To deter small parties (and especially extreme parties) a 5 per cent minimum requirement was introduced for allocation of list seats to parties, but with this minimum requirement calculated separately within each Land. Alternatively, a party with fewer than 5 per cent of votes but with at least one constituency seat would qualify for a proportional allocation of list seats in that Land. This 5 per cent Land-based qualification for list seats helped parties with local strength, but which could not secure 5 per cent of the total vote. It disadvantaged parties which would obtain 5 per cent overall, but would fall below that level in some Länder. Voters had only a single vote: the vote for a constituency candidate was automatically a vote for that candidate's party list, so split-voting was not possible.

The newly elected Bundestag had to pass a law to provide an electoral system for the 1953 election. Again arguments about the desirability of proportional representation, and the different ways in which such a system, if favoured, could be implemented, were rehearsed in the Bundestag committee dealing with the proposed law, and then in the plenary sessions of the Bundestag and in press and academic commentaries. The difference from 1949 was that this time the coalition of Christian Democrats, liberal Free Democrats and the conservative German Party (DP), possessed a clear majority in the Bundestag. However, as differences existed among these coalition partners concerning which electoral system was to be preferred, as well as between them and the opposition SPD, that coalition could not force through an agreed proposal but rather had to consent to compromises. The 1953 Electoral Law, partly because of pressure of time (the election date was drawing very near before the committee stage was completed), followed closely the 1949 electoral system. The only differences of significance were the separation of the constituency and list votes (thus permitting split-voting), an increase in the standard size of the Bundestag – not counting any surplus seats – from 400 to 484, of which constituency seats and list seats each constituted 50 per cent, and the requirement that parties obtain 5 per cent of list votes in the whole of the FRG to qualify for allocations of list seats (or win at least one constituency seat).

Sensitive to the fact that time pressures had prevented as thorough an analysis of electoral system issues as might have been desirable, the Bundestag began its investigation into a revision of the electoral system soon after the 1953 election. The FDP and the DP wanted a swift resolution of the matter, since they were needed to provide the Christian Democrats with its two-thirds majority to over-ride Bundesrat opposition to legislation, and they feared that, once such power within the coalition was lost, their leverage on the details of the Electoral Law would also disappear (Lange 1975: 589–91, 605). However, as the parties could not agree on any very different form of electoral system, they stayed with what they already knew. The Christian Democrats, at Adenauer's urging, did suggest that in future the proportional calculation of seats should be limited to list seats only, making constituency seats a kind of 'bonus'. This was called the 'Grabenwahlsystem': because of the ditch (*Graben*) which would separate the two types of seats. This arrangement would have restricted the troublesome coalition partner of the Christian Democrats, the FDP, to only about half the seats it would otherwise obtain, and probably make the party superfluous in relation to coalition formation. This led to a crisis within the coalition, and the suggested change was quietly dropped. The outcome of the legislative discussions was the Electoral Law of 1956. This law, with only a few minor changes, has applied to all

Bundestag elections since that date (though in 1990 in a special variant, because of reunification: see below). It retained the half-and-half mix of constituency and list seats and the two votes for each elector. It did, though, now require parties to win at least three constituency seats as the alternative to the 5 per cent requirement for allocation of list seats, though any party winning one or two constituency seats of course retained these.

In general, the system in terms of the basic mechanisms for converting votes into seats has been regarded as satisfactory by the parties and the public. Only one serious proposal for reform has been made since 1956. The formation of the 'grand coalition' in 1966 enabled the Christian Democrats to launch another proposal to reform the electoral system to the disadvantage of the FDP, whose withdrawal from the coalition in 1966 had led to the removal of Erhard as chancellor and the creation of the coalition between the Christian Democrats and the SPD. An expert commission was created by the Minister of the Interior, whose remit was to propose a different electoral system which would produce more stable government, with less need for coalitions. Fundamentally, this was a demand for a British-style system based on simple majority voting in constituencies. Such a majoritarian system had been promoted by experts such as Hermens, by some newspapers and journals and by the *Deutsche Wählergemeinschaft* (the German Association of Voters), a pressure group which developed the case for majority-based elections as a way of producing stable and responsible government (Lange 1975: 424–31, 516–17). The SPD calculated that, under such a system, it might be condemned to permanent opposition. For this reason, and to please the FDP (with which party it might need to form a coalition after the 1969 election), the SPD decided not to support electoral reform, and the issue was dropped. Indeed, the SPD was able to persuade the FDP to support the SPD candidate for federal president, Gustav Heinemann, in 1969 by promising to abandon any future support for electoral reform that would be to the detriment of the FDP (Baring 1982: 108–12).

There have been suggestions concerning changes of detailed aspects of the electoral system (mainly by political scientists rather than politicians): for example, that the two-vote system be abolished, with one vote counting for constituency candidate and party as it did in the 1949 Bundestag election. A more controversial recent proposal has been that the voting age should commence at birth, with parents exercising votes on behalf of their children below the age of majority (Reuner 2004). Apart from the political wisdom of this proposal, a number of practical and legal objections have been raised, such as the prohibition of the Electoral Law against transferring voting rights to another person, or the problem of parents agreeing on how to exercise the vote of a single child. The suggestion has even been made that each parent can use half a vote for the child (*Das Parlament* 17–23 September 2002)! However, there have been no significant challenges from politicians in recent years concerning the basic characteristics of the system. One reason has been the redundancy of the reasons for criticism of the system in 1956 and 1966. In those cases, the Christian Democrats sought to rid themselves of the nuisance of having to rely on the FDP to form coalitions, and the eagerness of the FDP to use its position in the coalition to insist on its own policies when these were not congruent with those of its larger partner. The FDP has since become a more reliable and less uncompromising coalition partner, usually campaigning at elections for the continuation of the government of which it is a junior partner: indeed, 2002 was the first Bundestag election since 1969 when the FDP did not campaign as a member of the governing coalition (and also the first time since 1969 when it refused to commit itself to a coalition preference in advance of the election). Additionally, there is less concern now about extremist parties using the proportional representation system to win Bundestag seats, whereas in 1966–68 there were anxieties that the NPD would build on its successes in Land elections and win seats in the Bundestag. Following the 1994 Bundestag election, there were cases brought before the Constitutional Court which challenged the constitutionality of 'surplus seats' and the three seat alternative to the 5 per cent requirement for list seat allocation, but the court held that both features of the system were constitutional (see below). Academic experts have from time to time come forward with suggestions to amend the system: by abolishing 'surplus' seats, by removing the three-seat alternative to the 5 per cent requirement[1], or by introducing a second list vote (the *Nebenstimme*) to count if the first-choice party list fails to secure seats. So, armed with this second preference list vote, a voter could vote for a small party in the confident knowledge that, should that party fail to obtain seats by not winning 5 per cent of list votes, the second-choice vote – presuming it is for a more established party – would count instead (Jesse 1985: 254–60). So far, these proposals have met with little resonance among politicians.

The special case of the 1990 Bundestag election

The collapse of the communist regime in the German Democratic Republic (GDR) in autumn 1989 had consequences for the German electoral system. The newly democratic GDR experienced its first and, as it happened, its last democratic general election to the People's Chamber (Volkskammer) in March 1990. The electoral system employed for that election was similar to that used in Bundestag elections, with two major differences. Each elector had only a single vote, which had to be given to a party list in the regional constituency in which the elector resided. There were fifteen such regional constituencies, with between seventeen and forty-eight seats each, providing 400 seats in all. Second, no artificial barrier to allocation of list seats was laid down, so any party or civic groups presenting a list which received about 0.25 per cent of votes (i.e.1 vote in every 400) would qualify for a seat. A special clause barred parties which promoted fascist, militaristic or racist goals, such as the Republicans, who had already campaigned in the GDR after the fall of the communist regime. Use of this fairly liberal form of proportional representation enabled newly founded democratic parties and other organisations such as Democratic Awakening (*Demokratischer Aufbruch*), Alliance '90 (a grouping of various citizen groups) and an electoral alliance of Greens and feminists to win seats. Each of these won fewer than 5 per cent of votes cast.

A Bundestag election was scheduled for January 1991. The processes which led to the reunification of Germany on 3 October 1990 meant that there was a pressing need to bring that date forward. Consequently, it was decided to hold the election on 2 December 1990. The question now arose: under what electoral procedure should this election be held? It might be unfair for the system used in West German Bundestag elections to be adopted without adjustment to the new situation, in which a large section of the country (eastern Germany) was still developing its party system. The March election to the Volkskammer had shown that newly established parties in eastern Germany would find it difficult to win 5 per cent of votes in the whole of the newly-reunified FRG, as would the PDS, the former ruling communist party. A first proposal, to allow parties in the two parts of Germany to link their lists, thus allowing small new parties in eastern Germany to win seats in alliance with larger West German parties, was rejected by the Constitutional Court as a result of complaints by the PDS and the Greens – parties which would not have benefited from this change. A different proposal was then brought forward, which was adopted for the 1990 election only. Under this system, the 5 per cent requirement for obtaining list seat allocations would apply *separately* in western Germany (the pre-reunification FRG plus West Berlin), and in eastern Germany (the territory which had constituted the

GDR, including East Berlin). This would make it easier for eastern German parties, with no hope of establishing a significant voter base in western Germany before the election, to win seats at least for the first four years of reunification. For that election only, associations which did not fulfil the normal legal requirements to qualify for recognition as a political party were also allowed to contest the election (as had been the case for the election in March 1990). In addition, the standard size of the Bundestag was increased from 496 to 656, to accommodate the enlargement of the state. This was cut back to 598 as from the 2002 Bundestag election, with eastern Germany losing twenty-six of the fifty-six seats which were abolished.

For the 1994 Bundestag election, the system reverted to that used prior to reunification: the 5 per cent requirement once more applied to the whole of the FRG. By then, small new parties had to some degree disappeared in eastern Germany. The Greens and Alliance '90 had merged in 1993 to form a joint party. Only the PDS, of the significant parties, seemed threatened by this reversion of the electoral system to its previous basis. It had found it difficult to secure voting support in western Germany to supplement its undoubted popularity in eastern Germany. In 1994, the PDS survived by winning four constituency seats, thus qualifying for proportional representation. In 1998 it managed to qualify twice over: by securing more than 5 per cent and by winning four constituency seats. However, for a variety of reasons (see chapter 5) in 2002 it failed to win sufficient list votes or to win enough constituency seats to qualify for a distribution of list seats, and was confined to its two constituency seats only.

The devil is in the detail:
the electoral system under review by the Constitutional Court

Two special features of the electoral system acquired new significance after reunification, and, in doing so, highlighted a number of other technical and legal provisions of the electoral system. These two features were the provision for surplus seats, and the by-passing of the 5 per cent requirement by parties winning at least three constituency seats.

Why was it not until 1997 that complaints about these features were brought before the Constitutional Court? Mainly because until reunification the number of surplus seats had been very small at any election, and never of a quantity potentially to affect the outcome (in deciding which coalition would govern, for instance). Nor had the three-constituency seats alternative to the 5 per cent requirement operated for any party since the 1957 election, but after reunification this seemed to be the way in which the PDS would retain representation in the Bundestag, where its presence could make coalition formation a more difficult affair, possibly making 'grand coalitions' the only feasible option.

On the issue of 'surplus' seats, the Land of Lower Saxony brought a complaint to the Constitutional Court, after an attempt by the Green party to bring a case before the Court failed because procedural time limits had been exceeded. The complaint was based on one anomaly. For parties which benefited from an allocation of 'surplus' seats, the number of votes needed to obtain each Bundestag seat was considerably reduced, thus breaching the constitutional requirement that the electoral system be 'equal'. The judges of the Constitutional Court, in their ruling in April 1997, were divided on the validity of the complaint. Four judges (all of whom had been nominated by the Christian Democrats) voted to reject the complaint, on the grounds that 'surplus' seats arose from the explicit provisions of the Electoral Law which provided for a personalised element in the system of proportional representation: the election of constituency candidates. Provided the number of such 'surplus' seats did not become excessive, and provided a system for periodically adjusting discrepancies in the population size of constituencies was adhered to, there was no problem. The other four judges (those who had been nominated by the SPD) supported the complaint. They regarded 'surplus' seats as inserting an unacceptable degree of inequality between parties into the electoral system. However, since in the event of a tie between sets of judges the existing situation remained unaltered, the continued existence of 'surplus' seats was allowed. Various remedies to eliminate or compensate for 'surplus' seats have been proposed, such as calculation of seats for parties on a federal-wide, rather than a Land-by-Land, basis, or the introduction of equalisation seats, as exist in many of the Länder electoral systems (Behnke 2003: 26–8).

The three-seat alternative to the 5 per cent requirement has also been approved by the Constitutional Court. However, it is not regarded by the Court as an essential feature of the electoral system and the Bundestag could amend the Electoral Law to remove the requirement. There has been a reluctance to appear to discriminate against a party already in the Bundestag (the PDS) by abolishing this alternative requirement. However, now that the PDS, following the 2002 election, does not have a party group in the Bundestag, reform of this feature of the electoral system could be undertaken quite easily.

Two categories of MdBs?

A frequent question asked about the German electoral system is whether the co-existence of MdBs elected by two different methods (the constituency 'first-past-the-post' method and the proportional list method) results in there being two categories of MdB once they arrive at the Bundestag. For many reasons, the answer has to be that there is no discernible difference, except for the few occasions when the constituency MdBs have to perform ceremonial duties in their constituency: opening a new hospital facility or heading a delegation to a ministry in Berlin on behalf of a firm or other organisation. There is in any case on the part of the electorate less of an expectation that the constituency MdB is somehow specially identified with the constituency, in the way that such expectations exist in the United Kingdom or the United States, though there is some evidence that constituency MdBs in particular are paying more attention to local representation duties (Klingemann and Wessels 2001: 292). The rights and duties of the MdB within the Bundestag are the same for both constituency and list MdBs. They receive the same remuneration. There are no bye-elections, so the death or resignation of a constituency MdB results in a replacement coming from the Land party list, just as it would should a vacancy arise through death or resignation of a list MdB.[2] Another consideration is also relevant to this question of whether two categories of MdB exist. Most MdBs elected from the list have also contested a constituency. Indeed, there is in some parties almost an obligation to be available as a constituency candidate before being considered for a hopeful place on the party list. These list MdBs may wish to contest the constituency at the next election, or at least be remembered in that locality when the next Bundestag election comes round. So those MdBs will nurse the constituency, try to be politically visible within it and represent the constituents as assiduously as the constituency MdB.

However, the parties sometimes view victories in constituencies as symbolically worthwhile. This extends to the smaller parties: the FDP's victory in Halle in 1990 was very much a matter for prideful boasting by that party, which had targeted the city (the birthplace of Genscher, the party's elder statesman) through the campaign and held its end-of-campaign rally there. There is also an organisational bonus to a constituency victory. The constituency offices of MdBs provide a valuable organisational resource for the federal party: a local centre for communication, a useful link to the Land party organisation, and so on.[3] Biedenkopf, then minister-president of Saxony and a former General Secretary of the CDU, claimed in a newspaper article following the 1998 defeat of his party: 'The loss of so many constituency seats therefore confronts the federal party with an enormous organisational task' (*Frankfurter Allgemeine Zeitung* 8 October 1998). Certainly where a party has few or no constituency seats in a region, as is the case with the Greens in eastern Germany, then a party can be confronted by a serious challenge to its organisation.

Notes

1 There are various anomalies connected with the two-vote system. For example, voters who elect a non-party constituency candidate or a candidate from a party with no party list in the Land in which their constituency is situated, do not have their list votes counted, even if they have split their votes and voted for, say, the SPD. However, voters who helped elect the two PDS candidates in Berlin in 2002 did have their second votes counted. Many of these would have been given to the SPD Berlin list (as voters assumed the PDS would not get list seats). These additional SPD votes could have kept the SPD, instead of the CDU–CSU, as largest party and, had there been no 'surplus' seats, could have meant that the SPD were unfairly entitled to the privileges of largest party (such as nominating the Bundestag president) simply because of these votes (Jesse 2003: 3).

2 Two kinds of special circumstances would qualify the statement that vacancies are filled from party lists. First, the extremely unlikely situation could arise whereby a constituency MdB was elected either as a non-party candidate or as a candidate for a party with no list presented in the Land in which the constituency was situated. Should that MdB die or resign from the Bundestag, a bye-election would be held to fill the vacancy (para. 48(2) of the Electoral Law). Second, a party which benefits from surplus seats in a Land is now prevented from filling vacancies from the Land party list until the surplus has been exhausted. So the SPD, which benefited from two surplus seats in Saxony-Anhalt, could only fill the third and subsequent vacancies in that Land from its party list.

3 In New Zealand, where one seat is sufficient to by-pass the 5 per cent requirement for proportional representation of parties, constituency victories are also regarded as valuable for providing parties with local organisational resources, as well as for profiling the constituency winner (Karp, Vowles, Banducci and Donovan 2002: 6).

3

Political parties and electoral politics

The role of political parties in electoral politics

Elections in democracies are structured by political parties, are contests between parties and their candidates and result in a party or a coalition of parties assuming responsibility for government. In Germany, the novelty of parties possessing constitutional status emphasises this relationship between parties and elections. Their responsibility to 'participate in the formation of the political will of the people' – a bland and generalised statement of obligation contained in Article 21 of the Basic Law – certainly applies to their role in electoral politics, even if it is not intended to be confined to that. The constitutional restrictions on parties, especially in relation to party finance, are also aimed largely at electoral politics.

This chapter focuses on three aspects of party participation in electoral politics. The first is the constitutional and legislative context within which parties exist at all in Germany, within which they shape their organisation and conduct their myriad activities and bounded by which they engage in electoral politics. The way in which parties have built on this constitutional and legislative status to become so pervasive a force within the German political process also is discussed. The second aspect is the selection of candidates: for both single-member constituencies and Land party lists. Third, campaign planning and organisation require attention, since they are becoming increasingly important in relation to campaign strategy.

The constitutional and legislative basis of the German party-'state'

There have been numerous diagnoses of the reasons for the failure of the Weimar democratic system to flourish or even, ultimately, to survive and for the success of the Nazi party in establishing a dictatorship by way of a constitutional, if not necessarily a very democratic, takeover of power in 1933. Most of these diagnoses would include some blame being placed at the door of the political parties. So when the drafters of the Basic Law in 1948–49 considered how best to protect their new democracy and prevent a second dictatorship from occurring, they decided to include an Article of the new constitution devoted to the regulation of political parties.

This Article 21 contained three paragraphs. First, parties were given the obligation of participating in the formation of the political will of the people. Parties could be freely established. They were required to be democratic in their internal organisation and make a public accounting of the sources of their funds (and, since 1984, also of their expenditures and property holdings). Second, political parties whose aims or whose members' behaviour posed a threat to the democratic order could be prohibited as unconstitutional by the Constitutional Court. Third, since these constitutional provisions were of a high level of generality, it was stated that details concerning those provisions would be regulated by legislation.

Such legislation was a long time arriving. Not until 1967 was a Party Law passed by the Bundestag and Bundesrat (upper chamber), which provided detailed guidelines concerning the legal status of parties (such as requirements for parties regularly to contest elections to acquire or retain official status as parties), their internal arrangements and the democratic rights of members. The Law also regulates party financing – the principal reason why the parties eventually got round to drafting such a Law, since the cosy existing arrangements for state financing had been successfully challenged in the Constitutional Court. Since 1967, there have been several major alterations to the provisions for party financing and state aid to parties, prompted by the revelation of scandals or misuse of existing provisions, by new notions of what is right and proper in relation to party financing and to demands presented by parties who think existing provisions are inequitable and that changes should be made (Gunlicks 1995). The Constitutional Court has also been an important influence, since its decisions have necessitated the revision, or even the abandonment, of legislation regulating party finance.[1] Even so, such changes have not affected the ways in which the parliamentary party groups (the Fraktionen) are financed from public funds, nor the ways in which auxiliary organisations, such as the party foundations, benefit from tax concessions and public subsidies (von Arnim 2001: 117).

The requirements of the Party Law concerning the legal status of parties is a two-edged sword. It conveys on parties which meet such legal

requirements various privileges, including the right to present candidates
and lists in parliamentary elections, enjoyment of special status in law (in
contrast to organisations, which are merely 'associations'), and protection against prohibition on grounds of unconstitutionality except
through a case being heard by the Constitutional Court (whereas other
associations can be banned by the Minister of the Interior under Article
9 of the Basic Law). However, the constraints associated with such status
are also important. The internal organisation of a party must meet certain
strict requirements about internal democracy. Members' rights are protected by elaborate mechanisms to prevent penalties or expulsion without
due process. Rules requiring the proper organisation of meetings and
other activities, such as selection of candidates for public office, must be
adhered to.

The Constitutional Court has been required on several occasions to
give verdicts on issues arising from the provisions of the Basic Law which
are relevant to electoral campaigning. As well as issues concerning allocation of air time for party political broadcasts (see below) and cases concerning the operation of the electoral system (see chapter 2), the
constitutionality of government-sponsored advertisements published
during campaign periods (1977) was settled, numerous cases affecting
party financing (e.g. 1958, 1966 and 1968) came before the Court, a case
in 1978 concerned the right of broadcasting stations to deny air time to
extremist left-wing parties, and a case relating to the EP election campaign of 1982 involving freedom of speech, in which a candidate of the
SPD had equated the CSU to the radical right-wing NDP, was decided. A
similar case was decided by a Land court in Mainz in 1998. It stated that
the TV station, SAT-1, had to broadcast a party political broadcast by the
Republicans, which claimed Adenauer and Schumacher, the respective
CDU and SPD leaders of the first years of the FRG, as witnesses in support
of the Republican party policy of excluding 'criminal foreigners'. The TV
station had wanted to prohibit the broadcast on the grounds that it would
invade the personal protection of those deceased politicians (*Frankfurter
Rundschau* 2 September 1998).

The Basic Law and Party Law are not the only legal constraints on
parties. The Electoral Law also contains sections which restrict parties in
various ways, such as the right to present candidates without first gather-
ing large numbers of signatures to demonstrate the serious intent of the
party, and meeting other requirements before the Electoral Commissioner (Bundeswahlleiter) will sanction the right of the party to engage in
an election. The 'internal legislation' (Standing Orders) of the Bundestag

has an effect on parties: in relation to their status as Fraktionen, the provision of the president and vice-presidents of the Bundestag and the financial and other resource provisions for Fraktionen, for example. The struggles by the PDS to acquire the privileges of a Fraktion when lacking the required quota of MdBs in the period 1990–98 is a case where such 'internal legislation' affected the way a party could operate within the Bundestag system. Another significant formal constraint has been the election campaign treaties by which the main parties have, from time to time, agreed among themselves to regulate the timing of types of campaigning (e.g. the display of posters), limits on negative campaigning and arrangements for adjudication of inter-party disputes. The first such treaty was in 1965. The allocation system for radio and TV party political broadcasts has been the subject of formal agreements among the Länder (responsible under the Basic Law for broadcasting policy) following a case decided by the Constitutional Court in 1957 which confirmed that political parties could be allocated different amounts of broadcasting time based on their importance, though new parties had to be given some allocation (Kitzinger 1960: 266).[2] The first such agreement was signed in 1961. A revised version in 1992 took account of the reunification of Germany and the growth in private broadcasting facilities (Holtz-Bacha 2000: 63–7).

Such legal provisions have the effect of conferring upon political parties the status of a fourth branch of government, alongside the executive, legislative and judicial branches. This in turn has led to critiques of such status, critiques which, in a country whose citizens have always had a somewhat ambiguous relationship to political parties, find a resonance which might be absent elsewhere in western Europe. Parties have even been accused of diluting the separation of powers in the FRG, through their influence over appointments to the Constitutional Court and patronage regarding posts in the civil service (von Arnim 1990: 28–9). The notorious press interview of the then federal president, Richard von Weizsäcker (Die Zeit 19 June 1992), summarised many of the misgivings which people had about the pervasiveness, unresponsiveness and self-serving behaviour of political parties. Their influence in the public service at federal, Land and local government levels, their key positions on the supervisory boards of broadcasting authorities and other public service institutions, the readiness with which they increased the salaries, pensions and allowances of their elected representatives, have all been criticised. 'The parties in our polity control (almost) everything, but who controls the parties?' wrote Robert Leicht (Die Zeit 19 June 1992). von

Arnim has developed a very thorough critique of the self-serving activities of 'the system', which is protected by a 'political class' drawn mainly from the political parties, a class which controls the rules of the political game concerning money, power, patronage and other political resources (von Arnim 2001). The parties defend themselves against such attacks by pointing to the unpaid volunteer activities of members, to the indispensable role they play in democratic politics and to the ultimate power of the voter, through the ballot box, to change governments and to decide not to re-elect incumbents.

Candidate selection in the FRG

The decision concerning which politicians are elected to the Bundestag is made by the voters. The decision as to which candidates are offered to the electorate and from which they then make their choice is made by the parties. So much for the formal procedure involved. In fact, the decisions made by the parties concerning selection of candidates are equivalent to election in well over half the cases at most Bundestag elections. The reasons are various: incumbency; the 'safe-seat' situation in many constituencies; the inflexibility of the Land lists once their composition and ordering has been decided by the parties.

It must be remembered that there are two different selection procedures by which parties choose candidates for Bundestag elections. In the case of half the standard number of seats (currently 299 of the 598 seats) each party selects its candidate to contest the election in single-member constituencies. The remaining 50 per cent of seats are filled from the Land lists of parties according to allocations made after the election. Constituency candidates are chosen by party selection meetings, consisting either of delegates from the branches in the constituency, or the membership as a whole. List candidates are selected by Land delegate congresses. Since these delegate congresses convene after constituencies have selected their candidates, they can take account of the need to 'secure' those candidates by ensuring that they are given safe places on the list. Normally, each place on the list is voted on separately,[3] using secret ballots. In theory it is open to the selection congress to make any decision it wishes. Usually, however, especially for the places on the list likely to offer a good chance of election, the Land party leaders will have negotiated a set of nominations which takes account of gender, regional and perhaps generational balance, which includes, where desired, representatives of interests associated with the party (prominent trade unionists in the case of the SPD, for example), which safeguards the election of favoured constituency candidates who might be defeated in the constituency contests and so on. So any successful challenge to one of the nominations for these top places could lead to the whole set of nominations unravelling, with proportionalities thrown out of kilter and possibly bitter floor contests for every place on the list with any chance of election (Roberts 1988b: 106–16).

Candidate selection tends to reinforce conservative tendencies in the structure of the Bundestag, because it places emphasis on incumbency and permits parties to 'reinsure' constituency candidates against defeat by providing them with secure places on the Land party list. In the period 1960–90, 78 per cent of candidates elected to the Bundestag were incumbents seeking re-election (though this did not necessarily mean that these candidates were re-elected for the same constituency or on the same Land list as before). The average length of incumbency was just over eight years (Boll and Römmele 1994: 544–5). It is exceptional for there to be a contest for nomination as a party's constituency candidate where the incumbent wishes to seek re-election, and there are usually few challenges for the top list places at Land selection congresses. However, there is a problem in estimating from the formal record how many incumbents have been 'de-selected'. An incumbent may realise that renomination is unlikely, and so decide not to submit to the indignity of a selection contest and probable defeat. Similarly, an incumbent may be refused a safe place on a party list, but be given a lower place, which is tantamount to 'de-selection'. This applies particularly to the smaller parties which, in any one Land, may expect few list places to be 'safe'. So the former Health Minister, Andrea Fischer, was not given a secure place on the Green party list in Berlin in 2002 so did not return to the Bundestag and, also in Berlin, failure to secure a top place on the Green list led Christian Ströbele to make intense (and successful) efforts to win his constituency seat which, had he failed, would have meant his exclusion from the Bundestag. Data for the pre-reunification Bundestag show that in 1953 48.3 per cent of MdBs elected were not incumbents, but after that the highest levels of newly elected MdBs were 30.64 and 30.12 per cent in 1957 and 1969, respectively. The lowest was 17.5 per cent in 1983 (Handschell 2002: 79–84). In 2002 28.7 per cent of MdBs were 'first-timers' (Feldkamp 2003: 8).[4]

The 'incumbency' factor is reinforced by the practice of placing constituency candidates in top positions on Land lists, so that if they are unsuccessful in their constituency contest they still return to the Bundestag as list candidates. For example, in North Rhine-Westphalia in the 2002 Bundestag election, candidates for the SPD on the Land list in places 3, 4, 7, 10, 12 and 13 were successful in winning their constituencies, so did not need to be elected from the party list, allowing others to move up the queue, as it were, and win list seats. The candidate at number 14 became, in effect, candidate number 8 once those six successful constituency candidates had been removed from the list. In Bavaria, list candidates for the CSU in places 2–4, 6, 9–14 and 18–23 won constituency seats, so had no need of list places. There were 1,248 double candidacies in the 2002 election. The SPD, for example, had 290 double candidacies, meaning that all but nine constituency candidates also had a list place (though not in every case one sufficiently high on the list to be hopeful of election). The CDU had forty-three constituency candidates without list places and the CSU twenty-six.

The availability of 'safe' seats, both constituencies and top places on the Land list, means that the parties can guarantee to many of its candidates that they will be successful, whatever the losses or gains made by the party in the election. This helps the parties plan the composition of the parliamentary party (Fraktion) and, if the party is to participate in the governing coalition, to ensure that potential ministers are guaranteed election (Roberts 2002: 232–41). For the FDP, the Greens and the PDS there is always the possibility of the party failing to attain the necessary 5 per cent of list votes to secure party representation in the Bundestag (as happened to the PDS in 2002) but, apart from that, these smaller parties also can count on a small number of list places being fairly secure. For the FDP and Greens this means at least eight or nine seats in North Rhine-Westphalia; three or four seats in Lower Saxony, Baden-Württemberg and Hessen and one or two seats in Berlin, Schleswig-Holstein, Bavaria, Saxony and Rhineland-Pfalz.[5] The PDS won just over 5 per cent of list votes in 1998, and won between three and eight seats in each of the East German Länder, so those could be regarded as 'safe' seats provided that party won at least 5 per cent of the vote. The Christian Democrats and the SPD possess a considerable number of 'safe' constituencies, where only a political earthquake could endanger the chances of the party's nominee winning the seat. In the two Duisburg constituencies, the SPD candidate won with 57.7 and 63.2 per cent of the vote, respectively, and these gave majorities of just under 30 per cent and nearly 39 per cent over the CDU challenger. In Biberach and Paderborn constituencies the CDU candidate secured 57.7 and 53.6 per cent of the vote, respectively, giving majorities of 31 and 22 per cent over the SPD rivals. The CSU has over twenty constituencies where its candidate can expect at least 60 per cent of votes cast, and majorities of between 25 and 35 per cent over the SPD candidates. However, this practice of ensuring that incumbents desirous of re-election can be more or less guaranteed election by use of a combination of safe constituency seats and safe list places means that there is relatively little infusion of 'new blood' into the Bundestag. In 1998 in Bavaria only eight out of forty CSU constituency candidates were not already MdBs, and of the nine candidates on the CSU list placed in the top twenty-five who did not also contest a constituency, only three were not MdBs (*Bayernkurier* 19 September 1998).

These attributes of the system of candidate selection has meant that the parties with seats in the Bundestag have been able to improve the gender imbalance that had previously been such a reproach to any claim that the Bundestag was 'representative' in terms of its social composition. In Bundestag elections until 1980, fewer than 10 per cent of MdBs were female. By 1990 20.7 per cent were female, and the proportion increased steadily until 1998, when 30.9 per cent of MdBs were female. In 2002, 32.3 per cent (194 MdBs) were female, with the Greens (58.2 per cent) and the SPD (37.8 per cent) exceeding this average proportion (Lees and Saalfeld 2004a: 157). The existence of party lists has enabled parties to ensure that a certain number of female candidates are elected, and reinsurance means that female candidates who fail to win constituency seats can secure election from the party list. In fact there are always far fewer female MdBs elected from constituencies than from party lists. The entry of the Greens to the Bundestag in 1983 began the process by which parties became more conscious of the necessity of selecting female candidates both in constituencies and for lists. Although only the Greens, the PDS and the SPD have moved in the direction of formal quotas, other parties have had to become more conscious of the need to reduce gender discrepancies in candidate selection, as they have in relation to party office-holding and choice of ministers at national and Land levels of government. In 2002, 29 per cent of all candidates were female, the same percentage as in 1994. By comparison, in 1957 only 7.7 per cent of candidates were female, and in 1976 13.9 per cent (Bundeswahlleiter 1994: 19; Feldkamp 2003: 6).

The fact that the Land party lists are fixed by the nominating party congress means that (unlike the lists in Bavarian Land elections, for example, see chapter 6) the voter has no influence over the ordering and cannot indicate a preference for any one candidate on the list. This consolidates party patronage, since local, regional or national party organisations can use placement order on the list as a sanction against maverick politicians, irrespective of what the voters would wish. Though this might seem to contradict the constitutional requirement that elections be 'direct' (by giving parties such control over the nomination process), the Constitutional Court has accepted the system of fixed lists as compatible with Article 21, which gives parties the obligation of 'participating in the formation of the political will of the people' (von Arnim 2001: 262–4).

Campaign planning and organisation

'Whoever wishes to conduct a campaign must be able to understand both processes, to combine politics and communication. It is not sufficient to know how to reach the voter; he must also know what he wants to say to him' (Radunski 1980: 23). Bundestag election campaigns are planned and organised at an ever-increasing distance from the date of the election. In some ways, it would not be far from the mark to talk of a permanent state of campaign planning. One expert claimed that the planning of the next campaign begins immediately following the Sunday of the preceding election (Wolf 1980: 103)! A more differentiated definition of an electoral campaign is: 'that period in the permanent competition among parties, in which the parties undertake additional organisational and programmatic efforts in order to win votes for themselves' (Timm 1999: 9). Taking that definition and focusing on the additional efforts made by parties, certainly some decisions about the campaign are taken two years ahead of an election, and one year ahead many of the parameters for the campaign have been decided upon. The FDP, for instance, had a framework plan for the 1976 Bundestag election accepted by the party's Praesidium in May 1975 (Beyer 1979: 91). Anticipating a Bundestag election in December 1990 or January 1991, the FDP Electoral Commission met first in September 1989 to begin planning the campaign. The preparatory phase for the famous 1998 'Kampa' concept of the SPD (see chapter 5) was undertaken in the first months of 1997, a year and a half before the Bundestag election in September 1998 (von Webel 1999: 15). The technical and managerial arrangements concerning location of the offices of the campaign team, the available budget and the engagement of advertising, public relations and opinion research agencies all require decisions well over a year in advance of the election. A more political decision for the main party in opposition is the nomination of a 'chancellor-candidate'. Sometimes there is pressure to make this decision very early. It allows the candidate to establish an image as a potential chancellor, to seek publicity and offer a programme. On the other hand, too early a decision may give hostages to fortune and even allow the public to tire of the challenger. Sometimes, too, a potential chancellor-candidate will emerge as a result of a victory in a Land election: Schröder in 1998 was chosen following his success in the Lower Saxony Land election. Strauss was chosen by the CDU–CSU parliamentary party group in July 1979 fifteen months ahead of the election in October 1980, defeating Albrecht, the minister-president of Lower Saxony, in a ballot. Stoiber effectively became the choice of the CDU–CSU as chancellor-candidate in January 2002, nine months before the September election date. Usually, though, the leader of the opposition party will claim the right to be the chancellor-candidate (as did Lafontaine in 1990 and Scharping in 1994).

It has become the norm for parties to engage the services of one or more commercial firms to advise upon, and implement, aspects of the election campaign such as advertising, public relations and opinion survey research. This practice dates back to the first Bundestag election, but has become more sophisticated, sometimes with 'beauty contests' among agencies hoping to be awarded the contracts by a party. This reached its height in 1998, when the SPD engaged eight 'partner agencies' to assist with different aspects of the campaign (von Webel 1999: 18–20). Though there is a limited degree of similarity in preparing advertising for a political party in an election and advertising for a consumer product such as cigarettes or detergent, there are also significant differences. Parties and agencies may claim that the degree of commitment to the beliefs and policies of the party stimulate the advertising agencies to better, more imaginative and more effective publicity. One staff member of Ogilvy Mather and Partners, talking of his work for the FDP election campaign in 1990, claimed: 'I could not create advertising for just any party. There must be a degree of emotion present. When I write copy, there is always a little blood mixed in with the ink' (*Neue Berliner Illustrierte* 22 November 1990: 18). On the other hand, what may be an advantage of commitment for those designing advertising and other public relations materials could be a disadvantage for opinion survey firms, where independence rather than sympathy is the pre-requisite. So parties may find that the data reported by survey agencies too closely allied with the client party can be less trustworthy than that obtained commercially through contracts with fully-independent agencies. The links between the FDP and its agency: 'Intermarkt' in the 1965 federal election has been cited as one instance of an excessively close relationship between the party and a survey agency (Busch and Lüke 1965: 117–18).

The financing of election campaigns is constrained by two factors. First, the party must decide what resources it can afford to devote to the campaign. In this exercise, it can give regard to the likely result. State subsidies to parties have been tied to election results, hence optimism about the result can encourage spending because debts can then be repaid immediately following the election. Second, the party must bear in mind the need to account for its expenditures, under the provisions of the Basic Law and subsequent legislation. The SPD 1998 campaign cost DM40 million (about £13 million), according to the party's official statements. This included payments to contracted agencies. However, it is impossible to calculate the true cost of an election campaign since the official cost figures given by party headquarters do not include Land or constituency local expenditures, nor the expenditures of persons or organisations who pay for newspaper advertisements supportive of a particular party, or who provide facilities such as meeting rooms or the use of vehicles to aid the campaign. A more difficult area is the aid provided by party-related foundations, such as the Friedrich-Ebert, Konrad Adenauer, Hanns-Seidl and Friedrich Naumann Stiftungen. In formal and legal terms, they have to avoid providing direct aid to the parties. In fact, it is difficult to differentiate some of their activities (such as conducting survey research) from activities which are campaign-related. Some of the activities of the Friedrich Naumann Stiftung were judged to have breached the law concerning such separation in relation to elections between 1978 and 1983. It lost its charitable status for that period, and had to repay tax concessions it had received (*Der Spiegel* 7 September 1987: 14). Changes to regulations governing party financing in 1993 led to an increase in direct mailing by the parties to raise money for the campaign through many small donations, rather than large donations where the donors would have to be named publicly (Römmele 1997: 122).

The parties utilise orthodox campaign methods, developed over many years and tailored to the political culture of the FRG. As early as 1949 the CDU (not yet formally a nationally organised party) attempted to co-ordinate the campaign speaking engagements of Adenauer and other leading politicians (Recker 1997: 295). However, over time the emphasis on particular forms of campaign publicity has changed. Kitzinger's classic account of the 1957 Bundestag election campaign made reference to posters, leaflets, campaign rallies and so forth, but also noted the importance of cinema advertising and the use of mobile cinema vans which the CDU in particular used to bring Adenauer's image to the local population in villages and suburbs (Kitzinger 1960: 117–18). With the spread of ownership of TV sets, the use of the cinema declined in significance. TV became an important medium for campaigning; it offered parties access through party political broadcasts (which already existed for radio broadcasting), invited appearances of prominent politicians as guests on talk shows, and gave the parties opportunity to set its agenda for TV through 'managed' news events. In the 1980s the '*Elefantenrunde*' – a pre-election talk show with the leaders of each of the 'relevant' parties discussing with a host various aspects of the campaign – became a feature of the later stages of the campaign. However, this came to an end when Kohl in 1990 wanted to deny to Lafontaine the opportunity to be compared to Kohl directly by the viewing public (*Neue Berliner Illustrierte* 22 November 1990: 22). A novelty in 2002 was the pair of televised debates between Schröder, the chancellor, and Stoiber, his challenger. Each programme was watched by an estimated 15 million viewers. Evidence suggested that, as in elections in the United States, such debates tend to reinforce, rather than change, the attitudes of voters, though they may have had a positive effect on turnout (Faas and Maier 2004: 301, 310–14). The spread of commercial TV and satellite broadcasting which took transmissions across national boundaries allowed parties to purchase advertising time to supplement their allocations of party political broadcasts.

Increased sophistication of campaign planning has brought about an emphasis on targeted publicity: posters, pamphlets, even mail shots aimed at particular groups in the electorate, such as young voters, pensioners, certain professions, the self-employed, single parents and so on (Römmele 1997). Telephone campaigning has become more widespread. The Christian Democrats and SPD used the telephone in the 2002 campaign to contact party members, to recruit them for campaigning and to ask them to themselves use the phone to win voter support for the party. The FDP made more restricted use of telephone campaigning, though when voters used the FDP 'hot line' to contact the party, this became a means of fund-raising as well as vote-gathering. The Greens, for financial reasons, and the PDS because the party did not think telephone canvassing proper, avoided this method. Whereas in Germany 'cold calling' by commercial organisations is prohibited unless a previous commercial connection with the person has been established, for political parties the constitutional obligation to 'participate in the political will of the people' has been relied upon to provide a legal basis for such campaigning (Knabl 2002: 14–15).

Technological advances have provided the parties with a new weapon in election campaigns: electronic communication through e-mails and the internet. The use of electronic communication by political parties dates back to the early 1990s. By the middle of the decade the parties had begun to set up 'virtual' party headquarters on the net: the CDU, FDP and SPD in 1995, the Greens in 1996 and the PDS in 1998 (Bieber 1999: 100). In the 1998 election campaign, methods of employing electronic communication were becoming quite sophisticated. The leading politicians in the parties, such as Schröder, Fischer and Westerwelle, had their own web sites, and the parties used the internet to communicate with party functionaries, party members and the electorate, with the SPD's 'Kampa' project in the forefront of these developments (von Webel 1999: 23–5). In addition to the parties, non-party organisations such as broadcasting and print media enterprises and educational institutions provided the voter with information about the campaign through the internet. In 2002, the use of the internet was even further advanced, matching the rapid increase in the percentage of the population with access to the internet: nearly half the population over the age of fourteen (Hebecker 2002: 49). The FDP in particular attempted, with some measure of success, to use the internet to attract donations, claiming that those who gave money to the party in this way would simultaneously be captured for the party as voters. A number of 'on-line' debates between politicians from the government and the opposition 'blocs' were mounted on the net, allowing interaction with members of the public. Whether or not electronic campaigning increases the degree of dialogue between parties and the electorate, it does offer the parties an instrument to escape campaign 'agenda-setting' by the mass media, which has been identified as a factor in the dominance of TV in election campaigns recently, in Germany as elsewhere (Gibson, Römmele and Ward 2003: 83). It is also, through the low levels of expenditure required, a cost-effective method of campaigning which can benefit smaller parties especially (Hebecker 2002: 48).

The development of the 'catch-all party' (*Volkspartei* is the term nearest to that in German) has brought with it the utilisation of 'voter initiative groups' (*Wählerinitiative*) to enable the party to benefit from the advantages of electoral support from particular groups in the electorate. Such groups are often headed by prominent personalities from the arts, sport or commerce, and seek to attract support from persons who are not members of the party. For example, Günter Grass supported the SPD in the 1965 election, when he made fifty-two speeches on tours organised independent of the party's campaign schedules, and again gave much-publicised support to Brandt and the SPD in the 1969 and 1972 elections (Parkes 1986: 134). In 1972 a well-co-ordinated Social Democratic voter initiative: 'Citizens for Brandt' provided a clear statement of the format and purpose of the movement. Its campaign literature stated: 'We are not an organisation. We are not party members. What are we? We are electors with a variety of professions, viewpoints and interests and with one great thing in common: we are for Chancellor Willy Brandt.' The writers Heinrich Böll and Siegfried Lenz and the TV newsreader Wibke Bruhns were among the prominent personalities associating themselves with that voter initiative. The FDP followed its successful relationship with a voter initiative group in the 1971 Baden-Württemberg Land election by ensuring that a similar group came into existence for the 1972 federal election campaign: the 'Action Blue Triangle' (*Aktion Blaues Dreieck*), which it helped organise and to which it provided a small subsidy, as well as meeting the staffing costs of its head office in Cologne. A number of prominent personalities associated themselves publicly with this organisation, such as Esther Vilar, who wanted to use it to attack the restrictive abortion laws of the FRG. The organisation remained autonomous, making its own decisions concerning the format and timing of publicity events, and even held its own pre-election congress in Munich a fortnight before the election (Abromeit and Burkhardt 1974: 93, 96–101). In 1980 the controversial selection by the Christian Democrats of Franz Josef Strauss as chancellor-candidate called into being several voter initiatives, such as 'Citizens against Strauss', 'Women for FJS' and 'Citizen Action Democrats for Strauss'. Citizen initiatives became a common feature of later campaigns, but usually attracted less media and public attention once the novelty value had declined. Nevertheless a few such more recent initiatives attracted special attention. One was the 'Initiative of the Middle Classes' in Hamburg, which placed a full-page advertisement in newspapers just before the 2002 election, in the form of a job recruitment advertisement for a chancellor, which, without mentioning Schröder by name, claimed the post needed 'a minimum of four years experience in the post' (*Frankfurter Allgemeine Zeitung* 18 September 2002). In the same election campaign a leaflet from 'Soldiers for Schröder', signed by numerous active and retired members of the armed forces of all ranks, was seen as controversial, given the non-political status of the armed forces.

Campaign strategy

There are numerous different facets of campaign strategy which a party must consider, but four in particular are usually regarded as being of paramount importance.

The emphasis which is to be placed, especially for the SPD and Christian Democrats, on the prospective chancellor and perhaps on other prominent politicians, is crucial. With the decline in party identification since the 1970s, many voters decide on how to cast their vote primarily because of this factor. In eastern Germany, where party identification has been slower to develop and where traditional milieux have not been available to guide patterns of voting behaviour, the personal qualities of prominent politicians such as Biedenkopf in Saxony, Bernhard Vogel in Thuringia and Stolpe in Brandenburg have produced strong voting support for their respective parties at Bundestag and Länder elections (Jörs 2003: 149–51). Even for smaller parties, personalities can be of great importance. The FDP made the decision in January 1972 (when the party expected the next election to take place in Autumn 1973) to portray only Scheel, the popular Foreign Minister, on its election posters (*Der Spiegel* 3 January 1972: 21). Other examples include Genscher's popularity for the FDP in the 1980s, the difference made by the absence of Gysi from the forefront of the PDS campaign in 2002 and Fischer's popularity and his 'coat-tails effect' for the Greens, also in 2002. The selection of issues which the party is to emphasise (and possibly issues which arise only in the course of the campaign itself, such as the Berlin Wall in 1961 or the Elbe floods in 2002) can also win or lose votes for a party. Then there is the decision concerning whether to adopt a defensive or aggressive strategy concerning the voters themselves. Should a party seek to hang on to its loyal voters and make sure they turn out in maximum strength? Or should it more boldly risk alienating some of those supporters by reaching out to new types of voter, as the SPD has done since the Godesberg Party Conference in 1959, and which it succeeded in doing with great effect in 1998? The fourth type of decision concerns prospective coalition partners. Should a party make any announcement concerning preferred coalition partners in advance of election day? Would it alienate some voters by doing so? Or lose more voters by not doing so? And what tactics, if any, should be adopted to promote that coalition choice?

Researchers tend to agree that, in Bundestag elections, there is a 'government bonus' and probably a 'chancellor bonus' in addition to that, and irrespective of party (Holtz-Bacha 1996: 17). The role of the chancellor or chancellor-candidate in Bundestag elections is therefore of great importance, and, with the 'Americanisation' of campaigning in the FRG which involves greater focus on the chancellor-candidates, of increasing significance. There has been an increase in volatility among the electorate and in the tendency among undecided voters to make up their minds late in the campaign. So the fact that voters perceive greater polarisation between the chancellor-candidates as the campaign continues, means that their voting decisions are likely to be affected by their preference for one candidate or the other (Schoen 2004: 341–2).

Looking back, it is obvious that Adenauer dominated the campaigns of 1949–61, both as an asset to his own party (though a controversial one in 1961) and as a factor in shaping the campaign of the other parties. The focus of CDU–CSU campaigning on Adenauer's personality, his image and his record as chancellor during the crucial first decade of the life of the FRG, demonstrates his significance to his party and his electoral popularity among the public. His challengers in 1949, 1953 and 1957 – the divisive Schumacher and the rather colourless Ollenhauer – could not compete successfully with Adenauer's charisma. In 1965 Erhard suffered by contrast with 'the old man', who was still chairman of his party, and because of his own lack of personal appeal. Meanwhile the SPD had brought forward Willy Brandt, lord mayor of Berlin, to challenge Adenauer in 1961 and Erhard in 1965, increasing the SPD share of the vote at each election. Brandt became chancellor in 1969, partly through his ability yet again to increase the SPD vote (though the SPD remained second to the Christian Democrats), but mainly because the FDP preferred a coalition with the SPD to rejoining a government led by the CDU–CSU. Since then, no unsuccessful chancellor-candidate has been selected a second successive time to lead his party as challenger in an election. The CDU tried Barzel, Kohl and Strauss between 1972 and 1980, before Kohl was elected by the Bundestag as chancellor following a constructive vote of no confidence in 1982. The SPD tried Hans-Jochen Vogel, Rau, Lafontaine and Scharping between 1983 and 1994, but none of these could defeat Kohl. The chances of Stoiber in 2006 again contesting the Bundestag election as the Christian Democrat chancellor-candidate are not high, following his failure to win in 2002. There is also the matter of the political renown of the chancellor-candidate. Whereas between 1980 and 1998 the Christian Democrats had chancellor-candidates who were nationally known (Strauss, then Kohl), the SPD had such nationally known candidates only in 1980 (Chancellor Schmidt) and 1987 (Rau). Vogel, Lafontaine and even Schröder in 1998 were 'local heroes', each associated with the Land in which he was or had been minister-president. This meant that they had to establish their images with the electorate during the campaign (Schoen 2004: 327).

The 'personality factor' is a complex one in itself, and is intertwined with other features of an election campaign. Since 'personality' can cover a variety of personal qualities, as perceived by the voter, it is important to distinguish between those relating directly to politics – such as competence in government, the quality of rhetoric, the projection of a style of leadership – and what some term 'unpolitical' qualities, such as personal integrity, physical attractiveness and an unblemished personal history (Klein and Ohr 2001: 219). The campaigns against Brandt because of his pre-war and wartime personal history and criticism of Schröder because of his several marriages are examples of these 'unpolitical' factors coming into play in a campaign. Criticism of Strauss in the 1980 campaign because of his role in the 'Spiegel Affair' or Adenauer's successful projection of authority are examples of 'political' personality factors. Although it is clear that election campaigns have become more personalised, it does not follow that voters are using the personality of chancellor-candidates as their sole or decisive cue when it comes to making a voting decision. While personality was a dominant feature of the campaigns in 1972 and 1998, the context of the campaign (such as German reunification in 1990) and the condition of the rival parties can be important contributory factors, alongside the personalities of the two leading candidates (Brettschneider and Gabriel 2002: 128. 132–3, 137–8, 140).

Of course campaign strategies, especially of the party out of office, may focus on teams of personalities rather than just the chancellor-candidate. Because Strauss and Stoiber were from the CSU, explicit publicity had to be given to the CDU leader (Kohl and Merkel) in the 1980 and 2002 elections. The campaign of the SPD in 1969 included alongside Brandt a whole team of potential ministers, such as Schiller, Helmut Schmidt and Alex Möller, under the slogan 'We have the right people', to convince the electorate that an SPD government would be competent. Scharping in 1994 was seen in party TV broadcasts and on posters with Lafontaine and Schröder as a 'troika', to reinforce the idea of a team of heavyweight politicians able to form a government. In 1998 Schröder was often portrayed in publicity with Lafontaine (at the time, the SPD leader).

The increased emphasis of campaigns on personalities seems to be driven by three developments. The parties choose to focus more on personalities, less on policy issues, than in the earlier years of the FRG. Voters seem more susceptible to campaign strategies concerning personalities than before. Third, and perhaps as a consequence of the other two developments, the mass media concentrate more on personalities than used to be the case (Wilke and Reinemann 2000: 65, 79). These developments reinforce the dominance of the two major parties, by presenting the election as a contest between the incumbent chancellor and his challenger.

The somewhat forlorn attempt by the FDP in 2002 to present Westerwelle, the party leader, as a 'chancellor-candidate' was not taken seriously outside the FDP itself. The Constitutional Court ruled that there was no constitutional issue involved in the decision by the TV companies to exclude Westerwelle from the televised debates between Schröder and Stoiber. Previous court decisions had confirmed the large degree of discretion which the TV companies had in such matters, so the exclusion of Westerwelle because he had no realistic chance of becoming chancellor was perfectly legal (*Neue Juristische Wochenschrift* 2002: 2939–40).

To what extent, then, do people make a decision how to vote on the basis of such 'personality' factors? It is one thing for respondents in a survey to indicate a preference for one or other of the two candidates for chancellor. Whether that preference is sufficiently salient to be decisive in relation to their voting decision – or even in relation to a decision whether to vote at all – is a different matter. A voter may prefer the chancellor-candidate of one party, but far more weighty for that voter might be a party's stance on some particular issue, or a more general reputation for competence in government. In 1994 a survey showed that Kohl had a substantial lead among respondents over Scharping, his rival. For the SPD, though, a general image of competence proved important for many voters, so the Christian Democrats did not win by as large a margin as the 'personality preference' responses would have suggested. The reputation of the party seemed to be in general the most important factor in voting decisions, followed by the impression made by the chancellor-candidate. Issues were in third place, after these other factors (Zelle 1996). For the 1998 election, when not only did a complete change of coalition result, but also a large transfer of votes from the Christian Democrats and to the benefit of the SPD, it seemed that a complex interaction of factors, involving the greater support for Schröder rather than Kohl among the electorate, the positive image of the SPD and the negative image of the Christian Democrats, and a generalised desired for a change of government, all combined to produce the outcome (Wessels, 2000: 61–4). In 2002 Schröder's advantages over Stoiber in surveys and his seeming victories in the two TV debates did not prevent large losses of voting support for the SPD nor an increase in voting support for the Christian Democrats. So though a party may be well advised to publicise its chancellor-candidate or other popular political figures, the ways in which those personalities can affect voting decisions is complex and not straightforward.

The role of policy-related issues in election campaigns is another complex puzzle. On the one hand, surveys can determine which issues the electorate find to be the most important (though whether respondents then cast their vote because of their view of parties' or politicians' competence in relation to such issues is another matter). On the other hand, the parties through their publicity and the media through their reporting may emphasise other issues, for a variety of reasons. So analysts have to return to the obvious fact that voting decisions are made because of a combination of factors, including the interplay of issues, party identification and the image of chancellor-candidates.

It has been clear since the nineteen-eighties that unemployment has become by far the most important issue among the electorate. Whereas in the 1980 election only 58 per cent named that as 'very important', in 1983 88 per cent and in 1987 81 per cent did so (Forschungsgruppe Wahlen 1983: 32; 1987: 39). The 1990 election had one main theme: reunification. Reunification brought in its train even greater problems of unemployment (especially in eastern Germany), so it is not surprising that that issue remained far ahead of all others for respondents in surveys. It was named as one of the most important themes by 66 per cent of respondents in 1994 (and by 75 per cent of eastern German respondents), by 85 per cent in 1998 and by 82 per cent in 2002, when a further 15 per cent thought that the economy – to which unemployment is closely related – was also an important issue (Forschungsgruppe Wahlen 1994: 50; 1998: 64; 2002: 40). Other issues such as internal security, immigrants and asylum seekers, environmental protection and education were named by under 20 per cent in these surveys at the time of the election.

It is rare for German parties in election campaigns to promote specific policy promises. Especially on posters, in leaflets and party political broadcasts, where the emphasis has to be on simple, brief messages, the parties tend more towards generalisations, to promise better management of the economy than their rivals, to do more for education or the environment – or, if they can, to point to their record in office as one of successful government. In this way, they persuade voters that they are the most competent choice in relation to particular policy areas. For example, in 1998 the SPD was regarded as the more competent party in combating unemployment (SPD 42 per cent; CDU–CSU 24 per cent) and on pensions policy (SPD 38 per cent; CDU–CSU 28 per cent). The CDU–CSU was ahead on the economy (CDU–CSU 37 per cent; SPD 33 per cent) and combating criminality (CDU–CSU 34 per cent; SPD 19 per cent). In the 2002 election campaign, the CDU–CSU was regarded as having greater competence than the SPD in relation to employment (38 per cent compared to 29 per cent) and the economy (36 per cent compared to 31 per cent) (Forschungsgruppe Wahlen 1998: 67; 2002: 44).[6]

Parties may attempt to manipulate the issues agenda to their advantage, as the Christian Democrats did in 1972, when they focused on issues of domestic policy, knowing that the obvious issue of Ostpolitik would attract votes to the SPD–FDP government. The smaller parties, whether as members of the existing governing coalition or not, may use particular issues to profile themselves, as the Greens have done with environmental policies and issues concerning gender, and the FDP with 'enterprise' issues, such as reducing taxation for small businesses and the self-employed. Whatever the decisions taken by the parties, the ability to be flexible, to respond to new opportunities (such as the Iraq conflict and the Elbe floods in the 2002 campaign) and to combat policy-related propaganda from rival parties, may make the difference between defeat and victory.

Another decision about strategy is whether to emphasise positive or negative themes – or, a similar way of putting it, whether to be primarily aggressive or defensive. Of course, all parties will use some mix of these styles of campaigning, but in particular cases a clear dominance of one or other of these styles can be observed. In 1953, 1972 and 1976 the Christian Democrats, in rather different contexts concerning the Cold War, used aggressive and negative campaigning against the SPD by endeavouring to associate the SPD with 'socialism'. The 1961 Christian Democrat campaign against Brandt and the 1980 SPD and FDP campaigns against Strauss similarly emphasised negative themes. Examples of more 'positive' campaigning were in 1957 and 1990 by the Christian Democrats, and 1969, 1972 and 1998 by the SPD. In 1957, when Adenauer's reputation was at its height, the Christian Democrats could conduct a campaign which emphasised his own and his government's achievements. In 1990 the swift and successful process of German reunification allowed Kohl to conduct a triumphal election campaign as the 'chancellor of reunification'. The 1969 SPD campaign could combine references to the achievements of SPD ministers in the 'grand coalition', such as Brandt and Schiller, with an optimistic message about reforms for a more modern Germany. In 1972 Brandt was able to emphasise his and his party's role in the Ostpolitik diplomacy which had seemingly brought about a degree of détente for Europe and improved relations between the two German states, even though by the time of the election campaign such issues had lost some of their salience for the electorate. In 1998, as well as the clever tactics of the 'Kampa' unit in countering negative campaigning by the Christian Democrats, Schröder as SPD chancellor-candidate was able skilfully to emphasise his respect for the attainments of Helmut Kohl with a reminder to the electorate that Kohl was getting too old for the job and that sixteen years of Christian Democrat government was enough; it was time for a change to a younger chancellor and a more vigorous government.

The SPD in 1998 had learned one lesson from 1994: to emphasise more the value of 'first' votes, for its constituency candidates. The decision to chase such votes, especially in thirty-two target constituencies, was made for several reasons: it would bring in its train additional list votes (even if not on a full 'one-for-one' basis, because of split-voting); it would, in certain constituencies in Berlin and the new Länder, help to resist competition for left-wing votes from the PDS; and it might result in a few 'surplus seats', especially in eastern Germany (*Vorwärts* January 1998: 8). Similarly, the CDU appealed late in the 1990 campaign for both first and second votes (stating on its posters that: 'The second vote is the chancellor vote') but only when it became obvious that the FDP would secure sufficient votes to return to the Bundestag.

Decisions in a campaign concerning coalition strategy have especially been a problem for the FDP. When the FDP has been in government immediately prior to the campaign, then it has always indicated that it would seek to continue with its larger partner as a governing coalition, even though in advance of that decision there have been arguments about whether such a pre-election commitment would be the best strategy. Such debate occurred, for instance, in 1980, where a Land coalition with the CDU in Saarland was in existence, but the decision was made to seek to continue in coalition in Bonn with the SPD. There were many, such as Möllemann, the North Rhine-Westphalia FDP leader, who were unhappy about the decision ahead of the 1998 Bundestag election to retain the partnership with the CDU–CSU, led by a tired and failing Helmut Kohl. In opposition, though, the FDP has on each of the three occasions apparently risked losing vote-share by deliberately adopting an 'open-to-both-sides' position, refusing to commit itself explicitly to a particular coalition. In 1957, after leaving the Adenauer coalition in 1956, the party lost vote-share and became irrelevant in relation to coalitions when the CDU–CSU secured an overall majority. In 1969, having left the coalition with the Christian Democrats in 1966, the FDP again adopted a wait-and-see approach, though Scheel (the party's leader) did give strong indications during the campaign that the FDP would prefer a coalition with the SPD if the post-election arithmetic permitted. Nevertheless, the FDP only just secured the 5 per cent of votes necessary for continuing its presence in the Bundestag. In 2002, the decision by the FDP not to commit itself to a coalition with the CDU–CSU in advance of the election is considered to have cost the FDP votes, and possibly sufficient votes to prevent a CDU–CSU and FDP coalition from taking office.

Recently the SPD and Greens have been regarded as a 'bloc' and as natural coalition partners (especially given the number of Land coalitions consisting of these two parties), though not until 2002 did the SPD match the Greens' pre-election commitment to such a coalition by making an explicit statement that it would seek to continue in government with the Greens. Since reunification there has been the continuing threat of blockage of any two-party coalition other than a 'grand coalition' by the presence of the PDS in the Bundestag. No other Bundestag party was ready to serve in a coalition which included the PDS (though the SPD in Mecklenburg-Vorpommern has done so since 1998 and a coalition was formed between the SPD and PDS in Berlin in 2001). Despite minorities in the SPD and Green party who would be prepared at least to consider forming a coalition with the PDS, surveys have shown that neither among the public, nor among SPD party members, would such a development find support (Hirscher 1997: 22–30). This has meant that the CDU–CSU and SPD have had to take a position concerning their readiness to enter a 'grand coalition', and on what terms. The outcome of the 2002 Bundestag election, in which the PDS failed to retain its place in the Bundestag as a parliamentary party group, suggests that probably this danger of a 'blocking' element in coalition calculations has now vanished.

Notes

1 A decision of the Constitutional Court in October 2004 struck down changes to the financial provisions of the Party Law which would have been disadvantageous to small parties. The Court ruled that such changes would contravene the requirements of the Basic Law that parties should be treated equally.

2 Another important case involved a Constitutional Court decision in 1962 concerning a complaint by the FDP about differential allocation of broadcasting time for the North Rhine-Westphalia Land election campaign by Westdeutscher Rundfunk. The Court decided that there was a considerable amount of discretion allowed to broadcasting authorities under the Basic Law, provided reasonable criteria of balance and proportionality were adhered to, and rejected the complaint (Kommers 1997: 215–17).

3 For places low on the list, offering little realistic chance of election, places may be voted on in blocs of, for instance, five positions.

4 The situation concerning MdBs who did not return to the Bundestag in 2002 is complicated by the reduction in the number of MdBs from a standard 656 to a standard 598, a reduction of 58 seats.

5 In 1998 and 2002 these parties won at least these numbers of list seats in those Länder. With a vote-share of 5 per cent any small party would probably win several seats in the largest Länder, and count on two or three seats in medium-sized Länder, depending on vote-share in each Land for that party.

6 This disadvantage of the SPD on the issue of unemployment was partly due to Schröder having previously given a hostage to fortune by claiming that if his government had not reduced unemployment significantly by 2002 it deserved to be replaced! Of course the opposition seized on that in the campaign as a propaganda weapon.

4

The public and electoral politics

Public participation – and non-participation – in electoral politics

Electoral politics involves the public in many ways. Outcomes of elections, especially in relation to the composition of coalition governments and the policies which such governments then feel free to pursue, clearly impact upon the public. In addition, there are two obvious ways in which members of the public can directly participate in elections. They may participate as candidates, activist supporters of a party or candidate, financial contributors to a party or otherwise as participants in an electoral campaign. Secondly, they participate as voters – or as deliberate abstainers. The decline in party membership in Germany over the 1990s, and the trend towards increased professionalisation of electoral campaigns, which reduces the reliance of candidates or party campaign managers on the variable and uncertain assistance of voluntary helpers, has contributed to the decline in voluntary activity in election campaigns since the 1980s. Paralleling this is the decline in voter turnout over the same period. From a high of over 90 per cent of the electorate who participated in 1972 and 1976, a low-point of 77.8 in 1990 – the first all-German post-1945 election – has been scarcely improved upon in the three Bundestag elections since then (with turnout between 79 and 82 per cent). This decline in turnout is not a trend confined to Germany: low turnout in the United States, France, Switzerland and the United Kingdom, for example, has provoked commentaries about a danger to democracy as well as academic and party-sponsored research into the causes of this decline, which has led to claims that the 'party of non-voters' is now the third largest in Germany.[1] This phenomenon of low turnout in Germany has prompted many experts to seek to explain its causes (Eilfort 1994, 1996; Feist 1992, 1994; Hoffmann-Jaberg and

Roth 1994; Kleinheinz 1998; Schoen and Falter 2003; Völker and Völker 1998).

Leaving aside involuntary abstention (a person intending to vote, but prevented from doing so by an accident, for example, or a sudden journey abroad), voluntary abstention arises from a number of causes. There are habitual non-voters, usually with a low level of interest in, and information concerning, politics. Such habitual non-voters are found especially and increasingly among the younger age-groups in the electorate, and among female more than male persons. When this factor is coupled with a low level of formal education, the tendency not to vote increases considerably (Feist 1994: 43). Social isolation, indicated by absence of links to social institutions such as churches, trade unions or cultural groups, and living in a single-person household, have also been identified as contributory social structural and demographic factors related to electoral abstention (Kleinheinz 1998: 177–9). Lack of interest in politics has been found to be one of the main motives for non-voting. An Infas survey in 1994 revealed that 38 per cent of western German non-voters in the Bundestag election of that year, and 25 per cent of eastern German non-voters, named that as a reason for abstaining. A 'Shell' study of German youth found that only 34 per cent described themselves as politically interested, and only 35 per cent would be certain to vote in an election (*Das Parlament* 17–23 September 2002). However, since level of interest in politics has increased steadily since the 1950s, it is difficult to blame this for the trend to lower turnout in Bundestag elections since the 1970s (Feist 1994: 37). It is interesting that 24 per cent of eastern German non-voters, and 20 per cent of western German non-voters could not name any reason for abstention! A survey by NFO-Infratest in 2002 found that 37 per cent of non-voters mentioned dissatisfaction with parties and politicians as their reason for abstention, 31 per cent the lack of a party to represent the respondent's views, only 13 per cent a lack of interest in politics and 6 per cent the impression that a person's vote had no influence (*Der Spiegel* 29 April 2002: 48). Dissatisfaction with democracy and lack of trust in political parties are similarly cited as reasons for refusal to vote (Völker and Völker 1998: 179–81).

For a variety of reasons, turnout in Bundestag elections in the eastern Länder have been always well below the levels of participation in western Länder, even though the democratic elections held in the GDR in March 1990 prior to reunification produced a high level of turnout. In 2002 80.7 per cent of the western German electorate voted, but only 72.8 per cent of the eastern German electorate. Bremen was the western German Land with the lowest turnout (78.9 per cent), but this was higher than every one of the eastern German Länder, including Berlin. The economic situation in eastern Germany, the mistrust of party politics, the feeling of neglect by what is seen as a western German-oriented governmental system: these are among the explanations for this marked reluctance of eastern Germans to participate in elections. This trend may be worsening: turnout rates in Land elections in Thuringia (1999) and Saxony-Anhalt (2002) were 15 per cent lower than in the previous election, and turnout among the eastern German electorate in the 2002 Bundestag election was 7 per cent lower than in 1998. In 2004 turnout declined further in the Thuringia Land election to only 54 per cent, 20 per cent lower than in 1994. (Turnout in Saxony in 2004 declined only by 1.5 per cent (but to the low level of 59.6 per cent), and in Brandenburg it increased by 2.3 per cent (but only to 56.6 per cent), which could have been due in both cases to the likelihood of extreme right-wing parties having good chances of election, and thus attracting votes from alienated voters who otherwise might have abstained.) However, in the Bavarian Land election in 2003 turnout decreased by over 12 per cent, and in Saarland it decreased by over 13 per cent in 2004, so the causes of this phenomenon of declining electoral participation cannot lie only in the eastern Länder.

Non-habitual electoral abstention is more difficult to explain, yet is on the increase. With such persons, who may vote in one election yet next time withhold their vote, longer-term factors which do not change from election to election – such as educational attainment, social isolation or level of interest in politics – cannot provide an explanation. The changing attractiveness of candidates or party programmes at an election may be one reason for such sporadic non-voting (Schoen and Falter 2003: 35, 39). What seems certain is that the extraordinary force of civic obligation in German post-war political culture which made voting a democratic obligation no longer has much influence on decisions whether to participate in elections or not (Hartenstein 2002: 42).

There have been suggestions that declining turnout (though turnout levels that still, be it noted, are well above the levels of turnout in national elections in several other European democracies, including the United Kingdom!) is the product of a long-term trend to 'normality', after the establishment and early development of democracy in the FRG. This normality reflects satisfaction with the political regime. Additionally, Bundestag elections usually seem predestined to retain a government in office, even if the composition of the coalition is modified; such continuity has been the case in twelve of the fourteen Bundestag elections since

1949. In such elections (and that of 1998, where the change of government was widely predicted) there is less incentive to turn out to vote (Hoffmann-Jaberg and Roth 1994: 133–4).

Voting behaviour

Though analysis of non-voting may be useful and interesting, most attention has of course been devoted to analysis of voting. Why do voters choose particular parties or candidates? Can factors such as social class, geographic location, age, gender or occupation give clues as to which party a voter will choose?

It is first important to be reminded that, in the German electoral system for Bundestag elections, voters have two, separate, votes: a vote for a constituency candidate and a vote for a Land party list. So voters may make incongruent decisions: in other words, they may split their vote between a candidate of one party (or none) and the list of a different party. Such split-voting is examined in more detail later in this chapter. Because of this feature of the electoral system, it is possible for voters to be unclear as to the relative importance of the two different votes. Indeed, at every election, even just before polling day a large minority of voters displays confusion about the relative importance of the 'first' (constituency) and 'second' (list) votes. It remains unclear why this should be a persistent problem in Germany, after fifty years of Bundestag elections and explicit programmes of voter education from, for example, the Federal Centre for Political Education (*Bundeszentrale für politische Bildung*). In New Zealand, for example, where a two-vote mixed-member system was introduced first for the 1996 election, surveys revealed a high degree of understanding from the outset of the different purposes of the two votes which could be cast.[2]

Understanding of the two-vote system may be linked to the level of invalid voting, since it might be expected that failure to understand how the electoral system works could lead to persons making errors that invalidate their votes. There are three forms of invalid voting: where the constituency vote, but not the list vote, is invalid; where the list vote, but not the constituency vote, is invalid and where both votes are invalid (Jesse 1985: 303–7). In 2002 1.5 per cent of constituency votes, but only 1.2 per cent of list votes, were invalid (with voters in eastern Germany casting higher levels of invalid votes than western German voters). These levels of invalid voting have been almost unchanged across the four Bundestag elections since reunification. Indeed, since 1972 the level of invalid voting has remained well below 2 per cent, declining from between 3 and 4 per cent between 1949 and 1957 and between 2 and 3 per cent from 1961 to 1969.[3] However, most invalid votes are only invalid for either the constituency or the list vote, and seem to arise from a decision not to use one of the votes, rather than out of failure to understand how to vote, so this evidence concerning a link between invalid voting and failure of comprehension of the operation of the electoral system is unconvincing.

Analysts generally use decisions of the voter concerning list votes (rather than constituency votes) for psephological purposes, and that will be the case in this chapter, unless the context makes it clear that constituency votes provide the basis for data. Even though many voters may not realise the greater significance of the list vote, for calculating the outcome of the election the list vote is almost exclusively the only vote which matters (the exceptions are where surplus seats arise, or where a party qualifies for proportional representation by use of the three-seat alternative to the 5 per cent requirement, as the PDS did in 1994).

The analysis of electoral behaviour in Germany needs to take into account two, probably inter-related, types of explanation. Voters may vote as they do because of membership of social or demographic categories, which in turn may be related to political cleavages (class or religion, for example). Such voting decisions may be explained in terms of self-interest (a party may be perceived as more favourable to women, or associated closely with Christian values, for example). Since many voters may belong to several such demographic groups relevant to their voting decision, they may be 'cross-pressured': that is to say, their class or occupational membership may incline them to vote for one party, but their religious affiliation for another. Voters may, on the other hand, make voting decisions independent of their membership of social or demographic categories. They may vote because of identification with a particular political party, because they are impressed by a chancellor-candidate or are unimpressed by the opposing candidate, or because the policies of a party or the record of the incumbent coalition are viewed positively or negatively (see chapter 3). There may even be some event or development during an election campaign which tips the balance: between the decision to abstain and the decision to vote, or between voting for one party rather than another. In Spain the 2004 Madrid train-bombings are considered to have contributed both to higher turnout than anticipated and to the unexpected victory of the Socialist party, and in 2002 the Elbe flood disaster undoubtedly helped to revive the electoral fortunes of Schröder and the SPD. Voters may decide how to vote based on a desire to support a particular coalition, doing this by voting for the smaller of the two parties in such a likely coalition, in order to ensure that the smaller party remains represented in the Bundestag. One such case concerned the FDP in the 1983 election, when its decision to leave the coalition with the SPD in 1982 – seen by some voters as a 'betrayal' – had caused the party to decline in opinion polls dangerously close to the crucial 5 per cent margin. Among the leaflets distributed by the FDP was an appeal: 'CDU–CSU 47 + FDP 4 = 47 (and no CDU–CSU government!) CDU–CSU 46 + FDP 5 = 51 (and a CDU–CSU & FDP coalition!)'. Such 'coalition voting' is undertaken almost irrespective of the policies or leadership of the smaller party, through what some commentators term: 'loaned votes' (*Leihstimmen*), from those who would identify themselves as supporters of the larger party in the coalition but are desirous of ensuring that the smaller coalition partner remains in the Bundestag. These types of explanation can be combined, by considering some to be persistent, longer-term influences (such as gender, religion, occupation and educational attainment), whilst others (attitudes to chancellor-candidates, issue voting) are shorter-term, situational factors. However, fluctuations from one election to another can reveal changes in support for parties based on demographic and social-structural factors, as well as those caused apparently by situational influences, such as campaign content. It is also important to keep in mind that explanations of voting behaviour which apply to western Germany (which has over half a century of experience of Bundestag elections) need not apply also to eastern German voters, where social class, religion and other socio-structural factors are less pronounced as influences on voting (Jörs 2003: 145–6).

For example, in the 1998 Bundestag election, neither the SPD nor the Christian Democrats apparently had any particular advantage among either male or female voters. According to a post-election survey by Forschungsgruppe Wahlen, the SPD had 41 per cent support in both gender categories, while the CDU–CSU had 35 per cent support in each category. In 2002, though, the SPD had retained 41 per cent of the female vote, but only 36 per cent of male voters; the CDU–CSU secured 40 per cent of male voters, and only 36 per cent of female voters. The Greens in 1998 were supported by only 5 per cent of voters in the forty-five–fifty-nine age group and 2 per cent among those over sixty years old; in 2002 the levels of support were 9 per cent and 5 per cent, respectively (Forschungsgruppe Wahlen 1998: 18; 2002: 51) Among blue-collar employees, the SPD declined from 48 per cent support in 1998 to 44 per cent in 2002, while CDU–CSU support in this group increased from 30 per cent to 37 per cent (Forschungsgruppe Wahlen 1998: 22; 2002: 56). These examples, however, also draw attention to longer-term trends. In the case of age-related voting, analysis needs to distinguish between life-cycle effects and cohort effects. In other words, young voters may have voted Green because they were young in 1983 and 1987. Fifteen years later, do the Greens retain the votes of those same voters who are now in their forties (the cohort effect)? Or have those voters been replaced by other voters in the under-thirty-five age-group (the life-cycle effect)? It would appear that here both effects are at work: voters in the lowest age-groups vote Green in above-average numbers, but the age profile of Green voters shows that many former Green voters, as they grow older, retain loyalty to the Green party. For the SPD, not only is the reduction in percentage of support among blue-collar employees bad news; the fact that such employees constitute a declining share of the electorate means that even a constant percentage of voters in that category would represent an ever-smaller aggregate number of voters in an election (given unchanged turnout). In 1950 blue-collar employees made up 51 per cent of the workforce; in 1970 that had declined to 47 per cent; in 2000 (and noting that this now applied to an enlarged FRG) it was only 35 per cent, while the white-collar section of the workforce grew from 21 per cent to 55 per cent between 1950 and 2000 (Forschungsgruppe Wahlen 2002: 55). To some extent, this structural disadvantage to the SPD is compensated by the greater readiness of white-collar voters to vote flexibly, and not be tied to a party through loyalty or party identification, and the SPD has been rather successful in wooing such voters from time to time (Gabriel and Brettschneider 1994: 14).

Similarly, the decline in church attendance has had a long-term effect on support for the Christian Democrats. In 2002, in western Germany the Christian Democrats still received 53 per cent of the vote among Catholics, but from Catholics attending church regularly the CDU–CSU obtained 73 per cent of the vote. Among those Catholics attending church occasionally, 50 per cent voted for the CDU–CSU (Forschungsgruppe Wahlen 2002: 66). A similar trend is observable in Land elections. In the Baden-Württemberg Land election in 2001, the CDU won 44.8 per cent of the votes, but 53 per cent among Catholics, 69 per cent among voters attending church every Sunday and 73 per cent among Catholics attending church every Sunday (Forschungsgruppe Wahlen 2001: 28). Since year by year fewer Catholics and Protestants attend church regularly, this high vote among regular church-attenders will represent a smaller and smaller segment among those voting. One estimate suggests that the CDU–CSU lost 6 per cent because of secularisation over the period 1953–1990; the SPD gained 4 per cent, with the Greens also benefiting (Gabriel and Brettschneider 1994: 15). The one consolation for the CDU–CSU to off-set this trend is that church-going voters are more likely to vote than others (Roberts 2000: 68–9). Reunification has also been important for religious-based voting. In eastern Germany far fewer voters have ties to the church: 66 per cent in eastern Germany did not acknowledge membership of a denomination, compared to 16 per cent in western Germany (Forschungsgruppe Wahlen 2002: 63). Of those with such ties, most are Protestant rather than Catholic, which means that the Christian Democrats must win votes in eastern Germany through the attractiveness of their policies or their leaders, rather than through party ties based on religious affiliation.

Social class has come to seem a rather rough-and-ready category within which to analyse German voting behaviour. Instead, type of employment, education and the public sector–private sector division have been found to be more promising sub-categories for analysis. Both the Greens and the FDP, for example, obtain above-average support among voters with qualifications for tertiary education, while the levels of support among these groups for the Christian Democrats and SPD in 2002 were below the overall percentage of voting support received. The public sector–private sector employment categories, which are so useful in analysing voting behaviour in recent elections in the United Kingdom and Scandinavia, seem less valid as differentiating categories in German elections. In 1998, for example, the SPD seemed to gain votes from both categories of employment. However, Green voters come predominantly from public sector employment: one survey found that 18.1 per cent of those in public sector employment, but only 7.2 per cent in private sector employment, supported the Greens (Elff 2000: 86, 91).

Location seems also to have an influence on the distribution of votes among the parties. While in western Germany the SPD and the Greens both increase their share of the vote as population density increases in constituencies, the Christian Democrats experience the opposite effect: the lower the density of population (in rural areas, for instance), the higher the vote for the CDU–CSU. The FDP vote-share increases with density, but only to a certain point: in very densely populated areas the vote is lower than in small and medium-sized towns (Forschungsgruppe Wahlen 2002: 101). There is still a north–south differentiation observable which, like the density of population effect, may well be related to other social phenomena such as the predominant Christian denomination and frequency of church attendance, or the distribution of industrial employment which carries with it higher levels of trade union membership, but also higher levels of unemployment. The SPD tends to be stronger in the northern Länder such as Bremen, Schleswig-Holstein and Mecklenburg-Vorpommern, the CDU and CSU stronger in Länder in the south, such as Baden-Württemberg, Bavaria and Saxony. For the PDS especially, the identification of its supporters with the party's perceived defence of eastern German interests makes the east–west regional divide electorally very important (see below). An index of difference between voting patterns in eastern and western Germany demonstrates how little the two areas have come to resemble each other. Summing the total differences in vote-share (taking account of abstentions) between western German and eastern German parties, the index in 2002 was 23.2 per cent. In 1998 it was 25.1 per cent, in 1994 24.2 per cent and in 1990 17.8 per cent (Arzheimer and Falter 2002: 28).

Experts on German voting behaviour seem to be generally agreed that, for whatever reason, party identification has been in decline since the 1980s (Radunski 1986: 35; Gabriel and Brettschneider 1994: 9–10; Zelle 1994: 68). Surveys found that, for western German voters, in 1989 73 per cent identified with a party in 1989, of which 28 per cent were strongly identified with their party. In 1993 only 61 per cent identified with a party, and of those only 18 per cent identified 'strongly' (Zelle 1996: 334). Party identification still influences many voters' decisions, but policies and the image of the chancellor-candidate now appear to have an increasing effect. A survey in 2002 found that, for all voters, party identification was named as most important by only 18 per cent, the leading candidate of the party by 29 per cent, but the policies of the party by 49 per cent. For SPD voters the top candidate was the most important factor (42 per cent); for all other parties policies were mentioned as the main influence (ranging from 54 per cent for CDU–CSU voters to 66 per cent for FDP voters) (Hilmer 2003: 215). Many voters who change their voting choice in successive elections switch from one party in a 'bloc' to the other, rather than switch between blocs. However, it seems that voters in eastern Germany are not only more likely than voters in western Germany to switching between two elections, but are also more likely to switch across blocs (Schoen 2000a: 205–8).

Voters are not only more volatile than in the 1960s or 1970s. A significant, if small, minority make their decision concerning which party or candidate to vote for only late in the campaign. In post-election surveys, it was shown that in both 1998 and 2002 64 per cent of respondents had made their voting decision a long time before election day. In 1998 14 per cent, in 2002 12 per cent made up their minds a few weeks before election day. However, 6 per cent in 1998 and 7 per cent in 2002 decided how they were going to vote only a few days prior to election day (Kornelius 2003: 71).

Explaining extremist voting

A special case of great interest to analysts of electoral behaviour in Germany is voting support for the extreme right. Of course this support is very variable: situational voting is obviously strong among such voters, since the vote for such parties fluctuates so much at times. For example, the DVU obtained 3.4 per cent in Bremen in the 1991 Land election, 6.2 per cent in 1995, but only 3 per cent in 1999, and in 2003 2.3 per cent. In Bundestag elections its support in the period 1990–2002 was almost non-existent. In Baden-Württemberg Land elections the Republican party secured only 1 per cent of votes in 1988, but 10.9 per cent in 1992 and 9.1 per cent in 1996, but then declined to only 4.4 per cent in 2001. In Bundestag elections it attracted only 3 per cent of votes in 1990 and 1994, and 1.8 and 0.6 per cent in 1998 and 2002. So growing unemployment, or a particularly intensive and well-funded campaign by an extreme right-wing party in a Land election can sometimes produce relatively high voting support (the DVU in Saxony-Anhalt in 1998, when it won 12.9 per cent, is an example). Voting for the extreme right can be attributed to support for a populist party by those who perceive themselves to be 'losers from modernisation' or, in eastern Germany, from reunification. Unemployment appears to play a role in producing such support in western Germany, but less so in eastern Germany. A subjective feeling that one's personal economic situation is worsening also is associated with support for the extreme right (Andersen and Zimdars 2003: 17). The successes of the NPD in Saxony and the DVU in Brandenburg in Land elections in September 2004 were also associated with protest voting against the proposed labour market reforms of the Schröder government. While opposition to such reforms was expressed by 59 per cent of respondents in a survey, 83 per cent of those voting DVU in Brandenburg and 84 per cent of those voting for the NPD in Saxony were opposed to those reforms (Forschungsgruppe Wahlen 2004c: 11). Working-class voters, voters without tertiary education and young male voters are other groups from which extreme right-wing parties can hope to attract support at elections.

For example, a survey revealed that in the 2004 Brandenburg Land election, the DVU won support mainly among males under the age of thirty-five, with low formal education qualifications (Forschungsgruppe Wahlen 2004c: 12). One anxiety which many have is that right-wing extremist parties might manage to combine, creating on the basis of Land election successes an expectation that such a party would acquire more than 5 per cent of votes and thus be sure to gain seats in the Bundestag. Such a party might then benefit from the disappearance of the 'wasted vote' argument and serve as a vehicle for protest voting. This could result in it gaining a blocking position in the Bundestag, preventing any coalition of other parties from possessing a working majority except for a 'grand coalition'. Potentially, this was the situation concerning the NPD in 1969, following a series of electoral successes in Land elections. The announcement in October 2004 that the DVU and NPD were discussing plans for a joint campaign in the 2006 Bundestag election led commentators to suggest that this could produce a similar situation to that in 1969.

In contrast, voters for the one successful left-wing party that might be classified as extreme: the PDS, are concentrated very much in eastern Germany (in 2002 the PDS won 16.8 per cent of eastern German list votes, but only 1.1 per cent in western Germany). Many PDS voters have a university degree; they are more likely to come from non-working-class occupations than blue-collar employment. Those who perceive themselves to be 'losers from reunification' are likely to vote for the PDS, as are those who are pessimistic about their personal economic situation (Andersen and Zimdars 2003: 16–18). In 1998, an EMNID survey among those likely to vote for the PDS found that the main reasons were: the PDS representation of eastern German interests (51 per cent); the strong social engagement and good local government record of the party (49 per cent and 46 per cent, respectively); the party programme and the fact that it was a socialist party (34 per cent and 32 per cent, respectively); and its politicians (31 per cent). 29 per cent and 27 per cent said they would vote PDS as protest against the government and western German dominance, and only 5 per cent as protest against reunification. 28 per cent claimed that their personal situation had worsened since reunification (*Der Spiegel* 3 August 1998: 32).

The phenomenon of split-voting

Split-voting is a special feature of German electoral behaviour. It has become more widespread since the 1970s, with an estimated 20 per cent of voters now splitting their vote by choosing a constituency candidate of one party but a party list of another: double the percentage of the 1970s, and four times the estimated percentage of 'splitters' in the 1960s.[4]

So two explanations are necessary with regard to split-voting. Why has the trend increased since the 1960s? And why does any individual voter decide on split-voting?

The increase in split-voting seems to be accounted for by the same factors which explain increased voter volatility and increased readiness to abstain from voting for any particular election. Social ties are weaker, and the renowned 'milieux' which involved voters in life-long patterns of loyal support for a political party (especially the churches and the trade unions) no longer have such potent or widespread effect. Party dealignment and an increase in 'rational' voting, where the voter considers carefully how to vote and may make a voting decision only very late in the campaign, also contribute to this phenomenon. Certainly there are indications that potential vote-splitters have a more accurate knowledge of the operation of the two-vote system. Of those who intended splitting their vote in the 1998 election, 54 per cent could correctly identify the second (list) vote as the decisive vote, compared to only 47 per cent among all respondents (Hilmer and Schleyer 2000: 177). Despite the persistence of large numbers of voters who do not understand the relative importance of the constituency vote and the list vote, there is a growing minority with an understanding of the potential effects of split-voting – an understanding fostered especially by those parties which may benefit most from such voting. Since 1969, the FDP has been skilful in its publicity designed to attract list votes from voters otherwise loyal to the CDU–CSU or SPD – especially, but not solely, when it has been the coalition partner of one of those parties. In 1980, for example, it distributed a leaflet one side of which appealed to supporters of the Christian Democrats to give their party list vote to the FDP, while the other side had the same message for SPD supporters. The FDP has benefited to some extent from voter misunderstanding of the significance of the 'second' (party list) vote: the lesser value associated with the word: 'second' suggests it is less important than the first (constituency) vote, so giving the second vote to the FDP might sound relatively harmless to a supporter of another party, who can still give the first vote to his or her preferred constituency candidate (Roberts 1988a). The Greens have also appealed for list votes, though in a less systematic and organised manner than the FDP. While these smaller parties have sometimes suggested to the voters that the list vote was the way in which they could vote for popular national political personalities such as Genscher or Fischer, the SPD and Christian Democrats have countered by emphasising that they need list votes as support for Schröder or Kohl.

It is more difficult to identify with certainty the reasons why any specific voter decides whether to split the vote. Survey questions may elicit responses which give particular reasons, but without any guarantee that these identify the real, sometimes subconscious, reasons for such voting behaviour. Certainly a considerable proportion of such voting must be tactical. So split votes may be the choice made by supporters of a small party (especially the FDP or the Greens) who do not desire to 'waste' the constituency vote by supporting the candidate of their own party, a candidate who has no chance of winning the seat. Alternatively, supporters of a major party may 'loan' their list votes to their smaller actual or potential coalition partner, but express their true loyalty by voting for a constituency candidate of their own party. In the 2002 Bundestag election, survey data revealed that 79 per cent of those voting for the SPD constituency candidate also voted for the SPD list. So 21 per cent did not, of which 13 per cent voted for the Green party list. This could be regarded as a vote for the existing coalition, since both parties had announced that they intended to continue in partnership after the election. Similarly, 88 per cent of those voting for a Christian Democrat candidate also voted for the CDU or CSU party list, but 6 per cent of such voters voted for the FDP list. Looked at another way, only 28 per cent of voters giving their vote to the Green party list in that election also voted for a Green constituency candidate, but 65 per cent voted for an SPD candidate. 47 per cent of voters choosing the FDP list allocated their constituency votes to the FDP candidate, but 35 per cent supported a CDU or CSU candidate (and 15 per cent voted for the SPD candidate) (Forschungsgruppe Wahlen 2002: 98).

A special case in the elections of 1994, 1998 and 2002 was the pattern of split voting affecting PDS candidates. The PDS in 1994 won a distribution of list seats only because it won four constituency seats; it failed to win 5 per cent of list votes nationally. In those three elections, in the constituencies which the PDS won (and in others where it had hoped to win) it acquired more constituency votes than list votes. This was because some voters loyal to the PDS but wanting to avoid wasting their *list* vote, gave that vote to the SPD list and, perhaps, because some SPD voters were prepared to help the PDS using their constituency vote, but without loss to the SPD because the list votes still went to the SPD.[5]

The rationale for the two-vote system was to allow voters to support candidates because of their personal attributes, irrespective of (and without detriment to) the party preferred by the voter. In some cases, this seems to be the case. Prominent politicians in constituencies often run ahead of their party's list in their constituency. Politicians who have represented the constituency in the Bundestag over a long period of time can also be beneficiaries of a 'personal' vote, though, as in the United Kingdom, this is not especially frequent nor is the effect reliable or very large. However, in a few cases the personal qualities of the candidate appear to make a difference. The victory of Hans-Christian Ströbele in his Berlin constituency in 2002, the first ever Green party candidate to win a constituency seat, obviously owed much to his personal attributes, including his radical reputation: he won 31.6 per cent of the vote, but his party's list secured only 23.2 per cent in that constituency. As well as personal qualities and benefiting from fear of 'wasted votes' from supporters of smaller parties, constituency candidates obtain advantage usually from an 'incumbency' effect. Taken together, the 'wasted vote' effect, personal qualities and incumbency tend to support the idea that there is a small but significant 'personal vote' effect in the German electoral system (Klingemann and Wessels 2001: 294).

In his thorough and influential study of split-voting, Schoen concluded that a number of voters who split their votes did so in an 'irrational' manner. They gave their first vote to a party whose candidate had absolutely no chance of winning the constituency seat, and the list vote to a major party. Others split their vote between a candidate from a small party and a party list of a different small party which had little chance of obtaining the necessary 5 per cent to qualify for a distribution of seats (Schoen 2000b). Such patterns are, objectively, clearly irrational, since the constituency candidate of the small party has no likelihood of being elected (so that vote is 'wasted'). However, if such instances of 'irrational' patterns of split-voting are considered to be random, perhaps arising from lack of understanding of how the two-vote electoral system actually works, then it is likely that a proportion of the apparently 'rational' combinations of split votes are also 'random', where a constituency vote is given for the SPD or Christian Democratic candidate and a list vote for the list of a small party. It is very possible that some of those combinations of votes are made by voters similarly unaware of the relative importance of the first and second votes. (Indeed, on the same assumption, probably some votes that are *not* split might also be random!). So any estimation of the percentage of vote-splitters who do so for rational reasons must take that into account.

Assuming 'rationality', assuming voters do claim to understand (even if sometimes erroneously) what they are seeking to attain by split-voting, what are the principal reasons for voters splitting their votes? One reason is to avoid wasting the constituency vote. Since 1961, only two candidates other than those of the SPD, CDU–CSU and PDS have won constituency seats: an FDP candidate in 1990 and a Green party candidate in 2002. Very few have even achieved a second-place position in a constituency. Thus the rational voter really has to choose between the SPD and CDU (or CSU) candidate if that vote is to influence the constituency result. So voters who support the FDP, Greens or other smaller party will sometimes split their votes in favour of the constituency candidate of the SPD or Christian Democrats. Evidence for this is found in the percentages of voters for the party list who also vote for a constituency candidate of the same party. In 2002 the percentages were: CSU: 92.0; CDU 92.2; SPD: 86.4. For the candidates of the smaller parties, the percentages who used both votes for the same party (i.e. did not split the votes) were: Greens: 32.6; FDP: 47.7; PDS: 70.9 (Bundeswahlleiter 2003: 85). A reverse reason is when a supporter of the SPD or Christian Democrats wishes to ensure the parliamentary presence of the Greens or FDP (by helping the smaller party to obtain at least 5 per cent of the list votes), or intends to strengthen the coalition partner, or prospective partner, perhaps to restrict the strength of the major party.[6] The idea that a split vote can be a vote in support of a particular coalition by voting for both parties (though widespread) is false, because normally only the list vote will influence the relative strength of the parties or of potential coalition partnerships, so every voter really only contributes to the strength of one of the potential partners in a coalition, irrespective of how the constituency vote is cast. In a few cases, split-voting may be a genuine attempt by the voter to reward a particularly effective or popular constituency candidate, especially one who has represented the constituency over several years. Prominent politicians may benefit from their fame and reputation by securing constituency votes from supporters of other parties. One example in 2002 was Angela Merkel, leader of the CDU, whose constituency vote (41.6 per cent) was over 5 per cent ahead of the CDU list vote in her constituency and whose 4.7 per cent increase in her vote made her the only CDU candidate in Mecklenburg-Vorpommern not to lose vote share in 2002 (which indicates that she did not just benefit from FDP split votes). Wolfgang Schäuble, former chairman of the CDU, whose absolute majority of constituency votes (52.9 per cent) was 6.9 per cent ahead of the CDU list vote and Peter Struck, one of Chancellor Schröder's closest allies and leader of the SPD parliamentary party group prior to the election (51.1 per cent, compared to the SPD list vote in his constituency of 44.3 per cent) were other examples.

There are two other, special, reasons for vote-splitting. The first concerns the PDS, especially in the elections of 1994 and 2002, when the PDS seemed to rely on securing three or more constituency victories in order to secure list seats in the Bundestag. In those elections, there were local campaigns to encourage split-voting: from the SPD to win constituency votes from supporters of the CDU and FDP especially, who could be assumed to prefer an SPD constituency victory to one by the PDS candidate, and from the PDS, appealing to supporters of other parties to use the first vote to ensure PDS Bundestag representation. Of course, in either case the list vote could still go to the party which the voter really supported; nothing would be lost to the voter's party in that respect. In 1998 the SPD encouraged Green supporters to give their constituency vote to the SPD, and some local Green party branches encouraged this, especially where the PDS or the CDU hoped to win constituency seats, in places such as Berlin, Cologne, Schwerin and Rostock (*Suddeutsche Zeitung* 23, 25 September 1998). Plans for a more formal pact in Jena in 1998, with the Greens withdrawing their constituency candidate but SPD voters being asked to give their list vote to the Greens, were abandoned by the SPD because of the radical policies adopted by the Greens' congress at Magdeburg (*Der Spiegel* 20 July 1998: 42). In 2002, Wolfgang Thierse, the SPD candidate and the president of the Bundestag until its dissolution, won first votes from Green party supporters in particular (Green party: 16 per cent list votes, 6.4 per cent constituency vote). This was partly the result of a local campaign where leaflets and stickers appealing for just this combination of votes were distributed, but also it seems he attracted votes from FDP supporters and those voting for lists of small parties. Such split-voting was to ensure the defeat of the PDS candidate (who won 26.1 per cent, whereas the PDS list obtained only 20.2 per cent), but also a compliment to Thierse's own reputation and political service. In 2002, 21.4 per cent of voters for PDS candidates voted for the SPD list, and 19.6 per cent of voters for SPD candidates voted for the PDS list (Bundeswahlleiter 2003: 83).

The other reason is to try to manufacture surplus seats (see chapter 2). Since such seats may arise from discrepancies between first-vote and second-vote percentages (e.g. a candidate may win a constituency with 40 per cent of first votes, yet the party may win only 35 per cent of list votes in that constituency), patterns of split-voting may add seats to a coalition which it would not otherwise obtain. However, since the behaviour of voters, especially supporters of other parties, cannot be predicted or controlled with sufficient accuracy, it is very difficult to secure such an outcome through split-voting.

An outmoded form of vote-splitting concerned constituency pacts. These occurred in 1953 and 1957, based on the decision by one party – often the Christian Democrats – to abstain from presenting a candidate in a constituency, in order to allow a smaller party to benefit from votes which such a candidate would have received, and thus win the seat. Under the two-vote system, the larger party did not lose the important list votes in that constituency. While the success of such pacts is clear in some cases, in other cases it either did not succeed as hoped, or made no difference to what the result would have been anyway (Jesse 1985: 281–7). Superficial and unofficial proposals since 1957 to secure the assistance of the FDP for a coalition by ensuring that they won three constituencies by means of the CDU–CSU or SPD not offering candidates in safe seats came to nothing,[7] as did a short-lived scheme to withdraw some Green and SPD constituency candidates in Berlin in order to prevent the PDS winning constituency seats (*Der Spiegel* 14 September 1998: 32). Nowadays the public would see through such a manipulation of the electoral system, the major party candidates in such seats would not readily step down and the more volatile present-day voters could not be relied upon to follow instructions, so the attempt would almost certainly fail.

Does split-voting matter? It certainly can affect the electoral result, by giving parties, and indeed coalitions, more or fewer seats, depending on patterns of split-voting and the consequential list vote shares which parties receive. It can have some effect on the existence of surplus seats, which may reinforce or diminish the majority which a governing coalition would otherwise enjoy. The main effect, though, is to give the FDP and the Greens (and possibly in future the PDS) representation in the Bundestag. Making the major (and probably unwarranted) assumption that if split voting were not possible, parties would receive the same pattern of votes for the list as they do for their constituency candidates, then the FDP on six occasions and the Greens on two occasions would not have been present in the Bundestag (though the Greens under that assumption would then have obtained seats from western Germany in the 1990 election!). The FDP had fewer than 5 per cent of constituency votes in: 1969, 1972, 1983, 1987, 1994 and 1998. The Greens had fewer than 5 per cent of constituency votes in 1983 and 1998. However, split-voting allowed supporters of the FDP and Greens to make a gift of their – otherwise useless – constituency votes to candidates of their potential coalition partner. Had the FDP and Greens needed such votes to attain the necessary 5 per cent for representation, then in most of the cases mentioned those parties would have secured at least 5 per cent of constituency votes also.

Electoral research institutes: their role in electoral politics

No election in Germany is complete without its panoply of surveys of electoral intentions, and its battery of research questions about important issues, the images of leading politicians and the popularity of the political parties. Such electoral research provides stories for the newspapers and broadcast media, guidance for the party navigators of campaign strategies and data for the academic researcher concerned with finding cause and effect in relation to electoral outcomes. Whether the results of surveys from research institutes reflect more than they affect voter opinion is a matter of continuing controversy.

Opinion surveys were undertaken by the occupation authorities in the period between the entry of Allied military units into Germany and the founding of the FRG in 1949. The Allied authorities wanted to know how well their policies of democratisation were succeeding, and the extent to which the propaganda of the Third Reich still influenced the attitudes of the German people. Once the FRG had come into being, the Germans themselves took an interest in conducting opinion research. Noelle-Neumann and Neumann founded the Institut für Demoskopie in Allensbach in 1947, for example. The Universities of Cologne and Mannheim in particular became centres of academic expertise in electoral research. The Cologne study of the 1961 Bundestag election was an important pioneering undertaking, and Rudolf Wildenmann and the University of Mannheim became linked with ZDF from the 1965 Bundestag election: a linkage that developed into the Politbarometer as a regular survey of voting intention and other political issues.[8] In addition to research for publication by private research institutes and academic studies based on opinion surveys, the political parties themselves commissioned research for electoral purposes. The FDP was the first in the field (1950), but was followed within a few years by the Christian Democrats and the SPD (Kaase 1977a: 459). Now parties tend to have close association with particular research institutes, such as Allensbach with the CDU and Forsa with the SPD. In 1980, one expert identified ten different purposes for which political parties could usefully employ survey research, ranging from pilot tests of campaign materials to analysis of speeches, from profiles of candidates and parties to post-election investigations (Radunski 1980: 29–32). By the 1980s a whole range of surveys from at least half a dozen different institutes were published regularly during election campaigns, with comparisons after the Bundestag election to reveal which institute came closest to forecasting the actual result. Some of these institutes were regarded as being closer to one party than to another, so – probably unjustly – the results from such institutes were regarded with a touch of scepticism. Newspapers and TV channels have close links to certain institutes: the ZDF TV channel with the Mannheim-based Forschungsgruppe Wahlen, for example, Forsa with the RTL TV channel, Infratest-dimap with the *Frankfurter Rundschau,* and Allensbach with the *Frankfurter Allgemeine Zeitung.*

A number of controversies have been associated with survey methods and survey results. In the 1965 election, there were accusations that the Allensbach surveys had been manipulated to benefit the Christian Democrats by suggesting a closer race than really was the case (or proved to be the outcome). This led to the recommendation by the professional association of market research institutes that, in the 1969 campaign, no survey results should be published within the four weeks prior to the election. However, such recommendations carried no force outside Germany, so publication of survey data in the foreign press meant that such data became available to the German public anyway (Kaase 1977a: 461–2). The famous 'spiral of silence' thesis is also associated with the Allensbach Institute: the idea that the predominant climate of opinion may result in the failure of some respondents to declare their true opinions, when these go against the dominant view. So there will be underreporting of such opinions in surveys, which may through a bandwagon effect have influence on electoral behaviour to the detriment of those holding such unexpressed views (Noelle-Neumann 1982). Because of the potential influence of opinion surveys on voting decisions, it has been suggested that there should be an external auditor to ensure that objective standards of sampling, data analysis and publication of results are adhered to (Kaase 2003: 7). The ability of the Allensbach survey institute to predict the outcome of the 1998 Bundestag election better than its competitors was claimed to be due to that firm's methodology which took into account split-voting in a way other surveys did not (*Frankfurter Allgemeine Zeitung* 29 September 1998).

The voter: always an enigma?

There are numerous problems concerning the analysis of voting behaviour. First, voters themselves may not know exactly why they used their votes in particular ways at any one election. So it is impossible for analysts to be confident that their explanations (often based on responses from those voters in surveys) are accurate. The use of aggregate data, even when, in Germany, such data are complemented by the availability of the representative electoral statistics (see Appendix 4), carries the danger that important changes within a category – a particular constituency, for example – may be self-cancelling, so may hide changes which have taken place among individual voters. For example, suppose that 5 per cent of former SPD voters change to voting for the CDU candidate in a constituency, but 5 per cent of those who formerly voted for the CDU candidate now vote for the SPD candidate: vote-shares would be unchanged, yet a high degree of volatility affecting 10 per cent of voters would have occurred.[9] The utilisation of panel surveys, tracking changes in opinion associated with specific respondents, can counter some of these trends. It seems that recall data (asking voters to remember how they voted) under-estimates the volatility of the electorate to a considerable extent, compared to panel data (Schoen 2000a).

Second, explanations of voter behaviour which might seem to have validity for a series of elections might lose such validity as time passes, because voters individually, and the electorate in aggregate, change their behaviour and acquire new reasons for making their voting decisions. The spread of TV, then of the internet, the process of secularisation, the development and spread of post-materialist attitudes in an increasingly prosperous society, changes in the images of political parties, structural changes such as reunification: these are examples of factors which may render earlier explanations of voting behaviour redundant.

Third, the weakening of long-term ties to particular political parties, whether based on group membership (the churches, trade unions, for example) or on family tradition or personal loyalties, has meant that increasing proportions of the electorate make their voting decisions on an election-to-election basis, often deciding on which party to support (or even whether to vote at all) late in the campaign. Reunification has in any case meant that eastern German voters are less influenced by longer-term factors such as trade union membership or membership of a religious denomination, even after fifteen years of freedom from the communist regime of the GDR (Forschungsgruppe Wahlen 2002: 50). The more widespread use of telephone polling (due partly to its lower cost) has contributed to the increase in the number of surveys of voting intention during a campaign. The greater volatility in the electorate and the growth in the number of voters making their decision only late in the campaign means that such survey results can have a considerable influence on how a large minority among the electorate actually cast their votes (Kaase 2003: 5). So explanations of voting behaviour which rely on socio-structural factors have to take into account this 'dilution' process.

Looking at the behaviour of the political parties (see chapter 3), it seems clear that they believe campaigns can make a difference to the outcome of elections, and not just in terms of ensuring that loyal supporters turn out to vote. The planning that goes into the construction of electoral manifestos, the expenditure of time and money on experts in public relations, opinion surveys and advertising, the appeals targeted at particular groups or occupations during the campaign, the rebuttal of claims or accusations made by other parties: all indicate that elections are more than a matter of assembling batches of types of voters to make an election victory. The mass media are also regarded as influential in affecting voter behaviour during a campaign. Party political broadcasts, the 2002 televised debates between Schröder and Stoiber, the line taken by news magazines or newspapers: these are examples of factors which parties and political analysts regard as contributing to voting decisions. Voters have to be wooed, and the outcome of the election may depend on shifts in voting behaviour of a relatively small percentage of the electorate.

Notes

1 Of course, there are some who maintain that abstentionism is merely a symptom of satisfaction, with the government or with the political system, and that even relatively high and increasing levels of non-voting should not be viewed with alarm, nor as a sign of dissatisfaction with democracy itself. Nevertheless, to take the United Kingdom as an example, a government whose majority in the House of Commons has been produced by winning, say, 38 per cent of votes on a 60 per cent turnout has managed to persuade only 22.8 per cent of the electorate to vote for it, which must be a matter for concern.

2 Ahead of the 1996 election, a survey found that 71 per cent could correctly identify the list vote as the more important vote. After the election 56.6 per cent could do so. In 1999 49.7 per cent of respondents before the election and 57 per cent after the election identified the list vote correctly as the more important vote (Vowles, Karp and Banducci 2000: 10–11). In Scotland a survey demonstrated that there were lower levels of understanding of the features of the 'Additional Member' electoral system used to elect Members of the Scottish Parliament, and that, indeed, understanding had declined since the first such election in 1999 (Curtice 2004: 337).

3 In 1961 an unusually large percentage of invalid list votes was cast (4.0 per cent,

compared to 2.6 per cent invalid constituency votes). This may have been due to CDU voters not voting for their party's list because of Adenauer's refusal to give up the chancellorship, which became an issue in the election.

4 In 2002 20.9 per cent of voters split their vote. In 1976 only 6 per cent, and in 1990 15.6 per cent, did so (Bundeswahlleiter 2003: 82). In the 1996 New Zealand election 36 per cent split their vote. In 1999 21 per cent of voters in the Scottish parliamentary election and 19 per cent in the Welsh Assembly election split their votes (Johnston and Pattie 2002: 586–7). In Scotland it has been estimated that 28 per cent split their vote in the 2003 election to the Scottish Parliament (Curtice 2004: 337).

5 For example, in 2002 (where surveys indicated that the PDS had little chance of securing 5 per cent of list votes) Petra Pau won Berlin Hellersdorf-Marzahn with 37.7 per cent, defeating the SPD candidate (33.7 per cent). The PDS won only 27.3 per cent of list votes. The SPD received 38.8 per cent of list votes. The Greens also seemed to benefit: they won 4.7 per cent of list votes, but only 2.6 per cent of constituency votes. A similar pattern was observable in Berlin Lichtenberg-Hohenschönhausen, where the successful PDS candidate, Dr Gesine Lötzsch, won 10 per cent more constituency votes than were given to the PDS list, while the SPD candidate ran 6.2 per cent behind the SPD list vote in that constituency. In other Berlin constituencies where the PDS candidate had some chance of winning the seat, the PDS constituency vote was between 4 and 7 per cent greater than the list vote.

6 Surveys have shown that some voters are unhappy with the idea of single-party government (even if that party is the one with which they identify). This may be because of echoes of the single-party dictatorship of Nazi Germany, or of the communist countries before 1990. The FDP campaign in 1957, for example, played on this dislike by emphasising the role of the FDP as a 'third force' (Kitzinger 1960: 155–6). A survey in 1980 conducted by the Infas organisation found that only 23 per cent of respondents wanted a government of either the SPD or CDU–CSU alone. More tellingly, only 13 per cent of SPD supporters wanted their party to govern alone, compared to 78 per cent who wanted to preserve the coalition with the FDP. Among CDU–CSU supporters 47 per cent wanted their party to govern alone: still fewer than half of such supporters (Feist and Liepelt 1981: 40). In 1980 (when Strauss was chancellor-candidate of the Christian Democrats) some CDU voters gave the list vote to the FDP to prevent Strauss, of the Bavarian CSU, from becoming chancellor. In 1983 this was repeated, to ensure that Genscher (of the FDP) remained Foreign Minister and that Strauss could not then claim that office for himself. A survey of Scottish voters found that, for devolved Scottish government, 54 per cent preferred coalition government to government by a single party (preferred by only 31 per cent) (Curtice 2004: 335).

7 For example, on 30 September 1969 Kiesinger offered the FDP three 'safe' constituency seats after the 1969 Bundestag election, to give the FDP security that

it would be returned to the Bundestag at the next election (having only just secured 5 per cent in the 1969 election). This was an inducement for the FDP to enter a coalition with the CDU–CSU rather than with the SPD (Baring 1982: 157).

8 The first broadcast of Politbarometer data was on 29 April 1977. Generally new survey data are broadcast every month by ZDF. The background and development of the Politbarometer project is described in Sprickmann (2003: 17–27).

5

Election campaigns, 1949–2002

The importance of election campaigning for the political parties and for the electorate can be illustrated by a brief analysis of each Bundestag election since 1949. This will draw attention to the changes which have occurred in campaign styles and strategies over the past fifty years. It will also demonstrate the crucial importance of factors beyond the direct control of the parties themselves: especially the context within which the election campaign takes place (the background of post-war reconstruction in 1949; student-led radicalism in 1969; the flooding of the Elbe in 2002), as well as short-term and longer-term changes in electoral behaviour.

So in this chapter each election campaign will be analysed in relation to the context in which it occurs, which may include the record of the incumbent coalition, the outcome of Land elections since the previous Bundestag election, the state of the economy, international events and changes to the electorate or to the electoral system itself. Each analysis will give attention to the campaigns of the parties – though, for reasons of space, only the most significant aspects will be given attention. Each campaign also produces an outcome, which may or may not be directly attributable to the parties' campaigning, so the formation of the post-election coalition government, and the consequences for the parties not in that coalition, will be reviewed.

The 1949 campaign: 'the last Weimar election'

As well as possessing the unique quality of being the first Bundestag election, the 1949 election occurred within an extraordinary campaign context. The physical destruction caused by the war, the resulting displacement of the population, influxes of refugees from the Soviet Zone and Eastern Europe, shortages of basic provisions, the psychic burdens of the failure of the Weimar democracy and experience of Nazi tyranny, the restricted sovereignty which the new state would be granted by the western Allies, and the fact of a divided Germany all contributed to a very disturbed political background for the election. The elections to Land legislatures and constituent assemblies had already revealed the regional strengths of the SPD and the Christian Democrats, and a developing anti-left wing bloc was beginning to appear, linking the CDU and CSU to the Liberals (under a variety of local names) and regional conservative parties. The electoral system devised in the Parliamentary Council (see chapter 2) gave emphasis to local and regional campaigning of parties, since the requirement of winning one constituency seat or 5 per cent of the vote in one Land to qualify for Land-level proportional allocation of seats encouraged local campaign efforts, and in any case where central party offices existed they were still poorly organised and under-resourced. No split-voting could occur, as the vote for the constituency candidate was necessarily also a vote for the Land list of that candidate's party. The sixteen parties which presented candidates in the election had all been licensed by the occupation authorities, as licensing did not terminate until January 1950.

Falter (1981) has called the 1949 election 'the last Weimar election'. This is because of the large number of parties contesting the election and the relatively narrow focus of most of those parties. He also asserted that the parties themselves, their behaviour, rhetoric and slogans were reminiscent of Reichstag election campaigns in the 1920s and 1930s (Falter 1981: 241). The SPD was still very much an old-fashioned working-class party; one of its slogans in the election was: 'Socialism is our goal.' The main messages in its campaign were opposition to Erhard's 'capitalist' social market policies,[1] and emphasis on the unity of Germany (Toman-Banke 1996: 114–19). Though the CDU could not yet properly be called a 'catch-all party', it appealed to Catholics and Protestants, and contained a significant 'Christian Social' strand in its manifesto, which attracted working-class voters in several regions. Among the significant campaign messages of the Christian Democrats was their attempt to label the SPD as linked to communism and hence to the division of Germany and the 'red menace', claims countered by Schumacher's assertion that the CDU was really the party of the Allied occupation regime. Reconstruction, the record of the centre and right-wing parties in the Economic Council which had presided over the beginning of the 'economic miracle' based on currency reform (a message conveyed by Erhard in his campaign speeches), and hopes of reunification were uppermost in the campaign. In Bavaria the CSU emphasised Bavarian issues and was a predominantly Catholic party. Politicians with a pre-war reputation, such as Schumacher (SPD), Adenauer (CDU), Maier and Heuss (FDP), had an advantage in a campaign with a paucity of mass media outlets and no TV. However, the SPD did make skilful use of radio to report speeches of its leading politicians. The SPD campaign was the most centrally organised, and made use of professional advertising and publicity experts (Holtz-Bacha 2000: 91). However, unlike campaigns during the Weimar years and unlike later elections in the FRG, election campaigns relied on local organisation, rather than a scheme prepared by a central party office, and party slogans varied from Land to Land (Toman-Banke 1996: 94).

The result of the election was a victory for the Christian Democrats, who were able with the FDP and the DP to form a coalition government. The SPD, relegated, though narrowly, into second place, had to go into opposition. The anti-clerical attitude of the SPD cost it votes among working-class Catholics in areas such as North Rhine-Westphalia. Its best results came in industrial urban constituencies. The CDU, as expected, won seats in rural, and especially Catholic, areas. The FDP had its best results in seats with large percentages of Protestant voters. Ten parties secured representation in the Bundestag, including the KPD. Turnout was 78.5 per cent.

The 1953 campaign: the dominance of Adenauer

The Christian Democrats entered the 1953 campaign with most of the advantages. They were the principal 'party of government', and an early 'chancellor-bonus' effect was visible because of the popularity of Adenauer. They spent far more on the campaign than the SPD, making use of a campaign train and publicity films, focused mainly on Adenauer. The leading SPD candidate, Ollenhauer (replacing Schumacher, who had died in 1952), was uncharismatic and failed to match Adenauer in terms of campaign skills. The SPD made a significant error in using a slogan: 'Statt Adenauer – Ollenhauer' (in place of Adenauer – Ollenhauer), as this only drew attention to the greater skills and popularity of the chancellor (Wolf 1980: 199–200). The economic policies of the SPD, continuing to emphasise planning and public ownership of key industries and services, were rejected by voters concerned to retain the advantages of Erhard's social market economy. The coalition parties benefited from the popularity of their reconstruction and foreign policy programmes, which had initiated the 'economic miracle' and protected West Germany from communism. The brutal repression of the uprising of workers in East Berlin in June 1953 emphasised the consequences of communist rule, and the CDU made pointed use of that event by its anti-SPD poster: 'All paths to Marxism lead to Moscow. Therefore CDU!' The FDP used a similar slogan: 'Where Ollenhauer ploughs, Moscow sows! Therefore vote FDP.' True, the CDU had not done especially well in Land elections prior to the Bundestag election, but this did not seem to affect the outcome of the campaign. Nor did the ruthlessness with which the SPD accused the CDU of being corrupted by donations from business enterprises. There was a new Electoral Law, to replace the temporary arrangements under which the 1949 election had taken place. Now voters had separate votes for constituency candidates and party lists. Parties had to secure 5 per cent of votes in the whole of the FRG (not just in one Land) – or win a constituency seat – in order to secure list seats. This change was disadvantageous to small and localised parties such as the Bavarian Party, and benefited the larger parties.

A series of electoral pacts with the DP and the Zentrum reinforced the clear victory of the Christian Democrats.[2] They won 172 of the 242 constituency seats, and almost obtained an absolute majority of seats. They were strong in most regions of the country, except in the north-east where the DP had its strongholds and in some areas of Hesse where the FDP was particularly dominant. The coalition of the Christian Democrats with the liberal FDP and the right-wing DP continued in office. The SPD lost vote-share compared to 1949. Hamburg, Bremen and Hesse were its strongest areas. The FDP had very good results in Hesse and Baden-Württemberg. Local agreements with the CDU in Hesse meant that some FDP candidates won constituency seats with CDU support (Luckemeyer 1980: 220). However, the obvious divisions within the FDP between a more right-wing faction and the moderates associated with Maier and the Baden-Württemberg liberals, combined with the colourless leadership of Blücher, reduced voting support for the party. Only six of the twelve parties which contested the election won seats. The KPD failed to return to the Bundestag. Turnout increased to 86 per cent.

The 1957 campaign: 'no experiments!'

Much of political significance occurred between the 1953 election and the commencement of the 1957 campaign. In particular, the FDP had withdrawn from the coalition in 1956, because of disagreements with Adenauer concerning the future of the Saarland, possible changes to the electoral system and his failure to take the FDP into account when producing policy initiatives. However, the FDP, rather than the CDU or Adenauer, seemed to suffer from this conflict, and its campaign attacks on the CDU–CSU for wanting single-party government did not seem to be of great benefit to the party. The CDU played on continuing public concern about the Cold War, and dangers to prosperity. Adenauer was, more than ever, the electoral trump card for the CDU, and his 1955 coup in negotiating the release of prisoners of war still in Russian captivity provided him with a big electoral advantage in 1957. The SPD, again led by Ollenhauer, failed to dent the popularity of Adenauer or effectively criticise the economic or foreign and security policies of the CDU–CSU. The CDU again spent heavily on the campaign, making use of cinema films and its own touring cinema vans (as did the DP and the FDP, though to a far lesser extent), as well as leaflets, speeches and print media advertisements to reach the voter, and emphasising its slogan: 'no experiments!' ('*keine Experimente!*') to appeal to the innate conservatism of the electorate in the 1950s. The FDP, bruised by its experiences in coalition with Adenauer, called in one of its slogans for votes for the FDP to prevent 'one-party domination', to suggest indirectly a similarity between a CDU government and the Nazi period (Toman-Banke 1996: 184). Radio and TV for the first time carried party political broadcasts, which had been allocated according to party strength, based on an agreement between the parties and the broadcasting stations in 1949. There were 13 million radio sets in Germany, and some 900,000 TV sets (Kitzinger 1960: 264–7). All the main parties now utilised the services of advertising agencies and opinion research firms. The electoral system had again been revised, in the form of the 1956 Electoral Law, and now required three constituency victories as an alternative to the 5 per cent share of list votes as qualification for list seats.

The election produced, for the first and only time, an overall majority of votes and seats for one party: the Christian Democrats. Despite this, Adenauer included the DP in a coalition government. The FDP, which had decided, to its own cost in terms of electoral support, not to state a coalition preference ahead of the election, unsurprisingly was not invited to join. The SPD again failed to advance significantly in terms of vote-share, and its electoral pacts in Bavaria with a small left-wing party (the Peace Union – FU) made little difference to the outcome of the election. For the first and only time, the Bavarian sister-party of the CDU, the CSU, won seats outside Bavaria: in the Saarland, which had just joined the FRG in time for the election. Though women had a lower turnout level than male voters, their persisting dominant share in the electorate (due partly to the effects of two world wars) meant that they constituted the majority of voters, a fact which helped the Christian Democrats. Turnout again increased: to 87.8 per cent.

The 1961 campaign: delaying the inevitable

Despite Adenauer's popularity and his authority as chancellor and party leader, his age was increasingly becoming a factor in electoral politics. He was eighty-five years old when he began the 1961 election campaign. He had failed to make provision for a successor to either of his political offices, and had earned criticism for his unworthy toying with the idea of becoming federal president when Heuss came to the end of his second term in 1959. Many in the CDU wanted Erhard to replace Adenauer, a change supported by some in the CSU and among the electorate. A key moment late in the campaign was the statement by Mende, leader of the FDP, that he would enter a coalition with the CDU–CSU only if Adenauer were replaced as chancellor. The SPD had Brandt, the young, dynamic lord mayor of Berlin, as chancellor-candidate, and the party, having taken steps to broaden its appeal beyond its traditional working-class milieu by adoption of the Godesberg Programme in 1959, had hopes of displacing the Christian Democrats as governing party.

Campaigning took on more than ever attributes of Americanisation: sharply increased campaign spending, more intensive use of radio and TV, more emphasis than ever on the personalities of the leaders of the main parties, and even an – unaccepted – challenge by Brandt to Adenauer to meet him in a televised debate, following the example of the 1960 Kennedy–Nixon debates (Holtz-Bacha 2000: 103). The erection of the Berlin Wall seemed to offer an advantage to Brandt who, as lord mayor of the city, could profile himself as sympathetic to the plight of the Berlin population. Adenauer, in contrast, was reluctant to pay a visit to the city during the campaign. The Christian Democrats sought to portray the SPD as a party which would not know how to govern, which was untrustworthy and which would endanger the security, the prosperity and the welfare benefits which the FRG enjoyed. They also used the press to plant stories defaming Brandt as an illegitimate child, who in his youth had abandoned Germany for sanctuary in Scandinavia.

The outcome of the election seemed at first to be very favourable to the FDP: it secured its highest-ever percentage of votes (12.8 per cent), compelling the CDU–CSU to commence coalition negotiations with Mende and his colleagues. Obviously the attempt by the FDP to turn the election into a plebiscite on Adenauer's continuation as chancellor seemed to have succeeded. However, Adenauer was wily, drawing the FDP into discussions on policy before issues of leadership and allocation of ministerial portfolios could be addressed. By the time the FDP came to insist on his replacement as chancellor, Adenauer had secured the support of his party colleagues for a further term as head of the government. Erhard was unwilling to mount a challenge for the chancellorship, and the FDP was faced with the embarrassing choice of backing away from coalition membership or abandoning its key demand. The party decided to enter the coalition, and managed to obtain from Adenauer a written promise to make way for a successor well before the next election. The SPD had improved its share of the vote with its more modern and inclusive image, but was still some way from parity with the Christian Democrats. Turnout matched that of 1957: 87.7 per cent. Only the CDU–CSU, SPD and FDP were represented in the new Bundestag.

The 1965 campaign: in the shadow of Adenauer

Adenauer having resigned as chancellor in 1963, following the controversial 'Spiegel Affair' in 1962, Erhard at last became chancellor, retaining the coalition with the FDP. However, Erhard did not impress in his role as leader of the government, and a variety of problems – relating to domestic and foreign policy – confronted his coalition.

The rather lacklustre campaign focused more on the chancellor-candidates than on policy differences, though the SPD did attempt to insert into the campaign discussion about social policies, including social security, pensions and education. For the first time, a 'treaty' agreed by the established parties sought to lay down rules about the use of campaign methods, fair treatment of other parties and regulation of disputes between the parties. A novelty was the initiative of the author, Günter Grass, who undertook a personal campaign in support of the SPD.

Erhard's reputation as creator of the 'economic miracle' was enough to give him the edge over Brandt. Though a close contest was forecast, in fact the CDU–CSU increased the vote-share obtained by Adenauer in 1961, obtained a clear lead over the SPD and so continued to govern in coalition with the FDP. The FDP secured over 10 per cent in Baden-Württemberg, Bremen, Hesse, Lower Saxony and Rhineland-Pfalz. The extreme right-wing NPD secured 2 per cent of the vote, and in some areas, such as parts of Hesse and Bavaria, received considerably greater support. Erhard formed a coalition government in which the FDP was again the junior partner. Despite Mende's own reluctance to make Strauss an issue, pressure from within the FDP and from some of its allies in the press to exclude Strauss from the coalition because of his involvement in the 'Spiegel Affair' led to acrimonious discussions during coalition negotiations (Mende 1986: 197, 200–2). Turnout was 86.8 per cent.

The 1969 campaign: time for a change?

The 1969 election campaign was unusual in many respects, not least because the two largest parties (the Christian Democrats and the SPD) entered the campaign as coalition partners but electoral rivals. This had come about because of the failure of Erhard to deal with the many economic and social problems which had arisen under his chancellorship. Nor had he been able to escape the shadow of Adenauer, who had remained as party leader even after his retirement as chancellor in 1963. A crisis provoked by the FDP led to that party's withdrawal from the coalition in 1966, and in consequence Erhard was replaced by Kiesinger (prime minister of Baden-Württemberg) as head of a 'grand coalition' government of the Christian Democrats and SPD. So in the campaign credit for successful policies was claimed by both these two parties, but both attempted to blame their partner for policy failures. In the campaign, the chancellor, Kiesinger, led the Christian Democrats, with Brandt, his vice-chancellor and Foreign Minister, chancellor-candidate for the SPD for a third time. The 'grand coalition' had been successful both in bringing the economy out of recession, though economic problems remained, and in preventing the radicalism of students and extreme left-wing groups from destabilising the political and social system. In addition the first tentative steps had been taken towards replacing the Hallstein Doctrine concerning the communist countries of Eastern Europe by a more flexible and realistic policy.[3] Proposals to change the electoral system to a majoritarian-based system had not been adopted (see chapter 2).

There were two other important factors in the campaign. The FDP had almost completed a change of identity from being a coalition partner for the Christian Democrats to being a possible partner for the SPD. It had changed its leader: Scheel replaced Mende. It had adopted a more radical set of policies, and had given its support in the presidential election earlier in 1969 to the SPD candidate, Heinemann, rather than to Schröder, the CDU candidate. However, formally the FDP refused to commit itself before the election to joining either major party in a coalition, though as election day grew closer statements indicating a probable preference for the SPD were made by some FDP politicians. The other factor was the extreme right-wing NPD, which had benefited from the combination of economic recession and left-wing protests to win seats in several Land parliaments in the period 1967–69. It seemed very possible that this party would obtain sufficient votes to overcome the 5 per cent hurdle and enter the Bundestag which, apart from anything else, might complicate coalition negotiations after the election.

The campaign saw further growth in use of TV for party political broadcasts, talk shows involving politicians and news about the campaign. The tendency for the parties represented in the Bundestag to employ external advisers, polling organisations and publicity firms increased considerably (Holtz-Bacha 2000: 110–11, 114). The Christian Democrats attempted to use Kiesinger's physical similarity to Adenauer to suggest, as one of their slogans put it, that 'it all depends on the chancellor', and to benefit from any vestigial doubts which the voters might have about the stability of an SPD-led government ('With security into the seventies' was one slogan used by the CDU). The CSU in particular attacked the SPD in its publicity, and made very explicit appeals to just those social groups which might be attracted to the NPD: farmers, the self-employed and refugees (Kaltefleiter 1970: 69–70). The SPD tried to promote the idea that, having had experience in the federal government, they could now be trusted to lead the government with new policies and a talented team ('we have the right people . . .'). The FDP, emphasising its change of identity, decided to present campaign materials in black and white, to differentiate itself from both its own past and from the other parties. The economy, policies towards Eastern Europe and the dangers posed by the NPD and left-wing radicalism were the main issues in the campaign.

Turnout was little changed from 1965: 86.7 per cent. The outcome of the election was, first, that the NPD had not won any seats so would not be a complicating factor in the arithmetic of coalition negotiations and, second, that for the first time since 1949 it was not clear which parties would form the government. The Christian Democrats had lost vote-share, but remained the largest party. The Christian Democrats had benefited from transfers of votes from former FDP supporters, though many former CDU–CSU voters now voted for the SPD or NPD. The Christian Democrat electorate in 1969 contained an above-average share of female voters, those from older age-groups, those residing in small rural communities, and church-attending Catholics. The SPD had gained seats, but remained in second place (though for the first time it won more constituency seats than the Christian Democrats). The SPD electorate contained above-average numbers of younger and male voters, blue- and white-collar employees, those resident in large towns and cities and those who did not attend church regularly (Kaltefleiter 1970: 158). The FDP had only just managed to retain representation in the Bundestag (5.9 per cent of list votes). No party wanted a continuation of the 'grand coalition', so this left the FDP as 'king-makers'. Though the FDP commenced formal talks with the Christian Democrats, the real negotiations went on with the SPD, and it was soon clear that, despite opposition from a minority within the FDP parliamentary party (including Mende, the former leader) a coalition with the SPD would be formed. This coalition seemed to be favoured by FDP supporters. In 1965 those who voted for the FDP party lists but who split their vote tended to give their constituency vote to the Christian Democrats. In Bavaria nearly 25 per cent of those who voted for the FDP list voted for CSU constituency candidates, but only 8 per cent for SPD candidates. In Hesse 19 per cent of voters for the FDP list voted for CDU candidates, 5.8 per cent for SPD candidates. In 1969, in Bavaria 12 per cent of FDP list voters voted for CSU constituency candidates but twice as many for SPD constituency candidates. In Hesse the figures were 7.8 per cent for CDU candidates, 26.6 per cent for SPD candidates. 51 per cent of FDP voters said in a survey that they wanted a coalition with the SPD, and only 32 percent a coalition with the Christian Democrats (Kaase 1970: 49–50). The FDP lost more voters to both the large parties than it attracted from them (Klingemann and Pappi 1970: 122). Scheel was made Foreign Minister and vice-chancellor, and the FDP had two other seats in the cabinet. The CDU–CSU, as the largest party, complained that a coalition that left them in opposition was illegitimate, and threatened to use Land elections to win seats in the Bundesrat in order to block government policies.

The 1972 campaign: the voice of the people

The election in November 1972 was unusual because it was the first premature election in the history of the FRG. The Bundestag was dissolved a year before completion of its four-year term because the governing coalition had lost its majority. The Christian Democrat opposition (despite its acquisition of renegade FDP MdBs) had been unable to demonstrate that it now had such a majority, when the FRG's first ever constructive vote of no confidence in April 1972 had failed to substitute Barzel, the CDU leader, for Brandt as chancellor. The election was the first in which eighteen-year-old citizens could vote.

The campaign was seen by the public partly as a referendum on the Brandt government's Ostpolitik, and its relations with the GDR. This helped the SPD, since more than two-thirds of the electorate approved of the Ostpolitik treaties (Kaase 1973: 158). The SPD emphasised the great contribution which Brandt, winner of the Nobel peace prize in 1971, had made to *rapprochement* with eastern bloc countries, but stressed that this was a patriotic development: 'Germans – we can be proud of our country' was one SPD poster slogan. The CDU–CSU (contesting an election for the first time as opposition party), realised that debating the issue of Ostpolitik was likely to be of advantage to the government, so focused instead on inflation and the financial situation of the country. Their chancellor-candidate, Barzel, failed to make much of an impact in the campaign, in contrast to his rival, Brandt. The FDP had completed its change of identity from a party associated with the Christian Democrats and a conservative version of liberalism to a 'social liberal' party, a natural coalition partner for the SPD. The unity of the party was reinforced by the decision of dissidents such as Mende to join the CDU or CSU, and by a more careful candidate selection process which either excluded completely candidates not fully supportive of the coalition with the SPD or reduced their chances of election by placing them low down on the Land lists. However, the FDP had been 'punished' by voters in Land elections for its decision to join a coalition with the SPD. In three Land elections held simultaneously on 14 June 1970 it had very poor results (5.5 per cent in North Rhine-Westphalia; 4.4 per cent in Saarland and Lower Saxony: in each case, a much lower share of the vote than the preceding or the next following elections in those Länder). It was heartened by a strong result in Hesse later in 1970 (10.1 per cent), which allowed it to enter a coalition government in that Land with the SPD. The televised debate among the leaders of the four parties represented in the Bundestag (CDU, CSU, SPD and FDP) – the so-called '*Elefantenrunde*' – was used for the first time in 1972. Brandt was seen as the most popular leader after that broadcast and Scheel ran ahead of Barzel and Strauss in terms of that performance (Kaase 1973: 162). The FDP gained support late in the campaign, and was strongest among tertiary

sector employees and in larger-sized urban areas. The Christian Democrats lost some support among one of its traditional clientele groups: older
women voters (Kaase 1973: 162–3, 165–7)

The election result was a public vote of confidence in the ruling coalition and a confirmation of the popularity of Brandt's *Ostpolitik*. For the
first time ever (and the only time prior to 1998) the SPD was the largest
party. The FDP increased its share of the vote to 8.4 per cent, safely above
the 5 per cent level, thanks to decisions made by floating voters late in the
campaign to choose the FDP. Whereas 89 percent of Christian Democrat
voters and 87 percent of SPD voters claimed in a survey to have made their
voting decision by October, only 53 percent of FDP voters had done so
(Kaase 1973: 162–3). Turnout was the highest ever recorded: 91.1 per
cent. Brandt continued as chancellor and Scheel (FDP leader) as Foreign
Minister. Barzel resigned as leader of the CDU in 1973, to be replaced by
Kohl.

The 1976 campaign: a contest of heavyweights

All three parties represented in the Bundestag contested the 1976 campaign under new leadership. Brandt had resigned as chancellor in 1974,
taking responsibility for the scandal resulting from discovery of a GDR spy
in his personal office (the Guillaume affair). Though Brandt remained as
party leader, Schmidt succeeded him as chancellor. Scheel had resigned in
1974 as FDP leader to become federal president, and Genscher took over
as party leader and Foreign Minister. Barzel had been replaced by Kohl as
chancellor-candidate and party leader of the CDU. The CDU, having held
a special meeting in January 1973 to identify the causes of its election
defeat in 1972, decided to focus its campaign on Kohl: 'the man that one
can trust', rather than on a team of leading politicians, and sent staff from
its campaign team to study the US presidential election in 1974 (Rabeneick
1979: 67, 71–2). The oil crises of 1973–4 and their consequences for inflation and unemployment, as well as an upsurge in left-wing terrorism especially through the Red Army Faction, meant that there was a mood of
insecurity in the Federal Republic. The CDU–CSU utilised this to their
advantage, through their slogan: 'Freedom instead of Socialism', developed from survey results, especially from Allensbach (Rabeneick 1979:
73). Against that, the claim of SPD campaign publicity that the government had created 'a model Germany' sounded rather hollow. The FDP
wanted to carry through a campaign based on 'the governmental, with a

whiff of opposition', so emphasised the importance of its four ministers in its publicity (the governmental) and had taken a decision ahead of the election to continue in coalition with the SPD, but stressed its 'liberal' identity as a corrective to the SPD (the 'oppositional') (Kaltefleiter 1977: 163). It also emphasised its independent identity in the campaign by appealing strongly for constituency votes as well as list votes (Beyer 1979: 92), a decision which led to its lowest second vote:first vote ratio since 1961 (it won 6.4 per cent of first votes, 7.9 per cent of second votes – a ratio of 1.23 second votes for each first vote).[4] It was helped in its campaign by popular perceptions of its unity. Only 31.2 per cent regarded it as a divided party, compared to 39.2 per cent who thought the CDU–CSU and 57.1 per cent who thought the SPD were divided (Kaltefleiter 1976: 16).

However, though the CDU–CSU obtained 48.6 per cent of list votes (their second best result ever), it was not enough to displace the SPD–FDP coalition, which had a majority of ten seats. Turnout was 90.7 per cent.

In constituencies with the highest proportions of blue-collar employees, the Christian Democrats (47.1 percent) managed to remain ahead despite the SPD improving their vote-share in those constituencies to 45.8 percent. Nine of the ten constituencies with the highest SPD vote-share were in the Ruhr area. The CDU–CSU continued to rely on high vote-shares in constituencies with the highest levels of self-employment (where it polled 62.9 percent) and with the highest shares of Catholics (63.4 percent for the CDU–CSU) (Forschungsgruppe Wahlen, 1976: 62–5, 76).

Six weeks after the election the CSU took a decision not to continue as partner with the CDU in a combined parliamentary party in the Bundestag (which had existed since 1949). Following a threat by the CDU to establish a Land party organisation in Bavaria, the CSU reversed that decision three weeks later. Meanwhile Schmidt had formed his new coalition govenment with few problems relating to either policy issues or the distribution of ministries between the parties.

The 1980 campaign: Strauss saves the SPD–FDP coalition

By the time preparations commenced for the 1980 campaign, it was clear that the SPD–FDP coalition was in trouble. The economic situation had continued to deteriorate, and the changes hoped for as a consequence of improved relations with the USSR and Eastern Europe had been disappointing. Land election results in the two years prior to the Bundestag election had, however, been favourable for the SPD, an unusual trend, since governing parties usually do not have good results in Land elections (see chapter 6). A factor of uncertainty was the decision by the Greens, following some successes in Land elections, to contest the election: would this siphon votes away from the SPD? The most remarkable pre-campaign event was the decision by the Christian Democrats to select the CSU leader, Strauss, as chancellor-candidate (the first time the Bavarian sister-party of the CDU had been given this honour). Strauss was a controversial figure, strongly supported in Bavaria and other parts of the south, but regarded with suspicion and hostility in the northern Länder. The feud between the FDP and Strauss since the 'Spiegel affair' in 1962 meant that there would now be no question of the FDP joining with the CDU–CSU in coalition after the election. This was reflected in FDP publicity. One poster read: 'For the Schmidt–Genscher government. Against single-party government. Against Strauss.' The uncompromising campaign by Strauss did not help the Christian Democratic cause. 'Vote for Strauss. Stop socialism' was one slogan his party, the CSU, employed.

In an election where turnout declined slightly to 88.6 per cent, the result was a loss of votes for the Christian Democrats, a very small increase for the SPD and a considerable increase for the FDP from 7.9 per cent in 1976 to 10.6 per cent. This increase for the FDP came from vote-switchers from the CDU and SPD, as well as from first-time voters, counter-balanced by small losses to the Greens and non-voters and from split-voting by supporters of both the major parties: Christian Democrats who supported their local candidate but could not vote to elect Strauss as chancellor,[5] and SPD voters concerned to ensure that the FDP remained in the Bundestag (Feist and Liepelt 1981: 53–5). The Greens secured only a very disappointing 1.5 per cent of list votes. The strong feelings of voters regarding Strauss as chancellor-candidate led to more striking regional differences than in previous elections. The CSU lost relatively few votes in Bavaria, but the CDU had large losses in northern Länder such as Lower Saxony, and lost vote-share in those Länder irrespective of social class or denominational distinctions (Feist and Liepelt 1981: 50). The SPD–FDP coalition continued in office, though the strains between the two parties meant that there were doubts about the ability of the coalition to survive for very long.

The 1983 campaign: confirmation of a change of direction

The strains already apparent in the SPD–FDP coalition even before the 1980 election had worsened by 1982, when differences between Schmidt and the left wing of the SPD compounded the friction within the coalition. The FDP finally decided that they should abandon the coalition, and supported the Christian Democrats in a constructive vote of no confidence, by which Kohl replaced Schmidt as chancellor in October 1982. Kohl realised that it would be advisable to obtain the sanction of the electorate for this mid-term change of government, so the second premature election in the history of the FRG was scheduled for March 1983. Schmidt decided not to be the chancellor-candidate of the SPD; Vogel, formerly lord mayor of Munich (and very briefly of Berlin) carried the standard of the SPD in his place.

The FDP campaign emphasised that it, and especially its highly-esteemed Foreign Minister and party leader, Genscher, would guarantee continuity in the new government. However, the FDP campaign was damaged by criticism of its abandonment of the coalition with the SPD, especially from disaffected FDP politicians such as Verheugen, formerly the FDP General-Secretary, and Matthäus-Maier, who had both decided to seek re-election to the Bundestag as SPD candidates. They claimed that the FDP had 'betrayed' Schmidt and the coalition. In a Land election in Hesse in September 1982, even before the constructive vote of no confidence, the FDP's departure from the coalition in Bonn with the SPD, and the intention of the Hesse FDP to seek a coalition in that Land with the CDU, led to a dramatic loss of voting support for the FDP: it gained only 3.1 per cent, less than half its vote-share in the previous Land election. To meet this accusation of 'betrayal' head-on and put a positive spin on their decision to change coalition partners, the FDP used the slogan: 'Freedom requires courage.' The Christian Democrats played on the worsening economic situation, promising a change of direction (the 'Wende') as well as improved domestic security. The SPD sought to conceal problems of party disunity and tried to frighten voters by indicating that the right-wing coalition would rob voters of the social benefits upon which they had come to rely.

The new coalition achieved the result it wanted: support by a majority of the electorate. The FDP, despite loss of vote-share, returned to the Bundestag, thanks largely to 'loaned' votes from supporters of the Christian Democrats, who wanted to ensure that their coalition partner had sufficient support to remain in the Bundestag. The Greens entered the Bundestag for the first time, partly by attracting votes from former SPD supporters. The SPD declined to 38.2 per cent, its worst result since 1961. Turnout was 89.1 per cent. The new government was formed but excluded Strauss (leader of the CSU), whose demand that he should be Foreign Minister was rejected by Kohl as well as the FDP.

The CDU ran ahead of the SPD in those areas with the largest percentages of blue-collar employees in the electorate (in 1980 the SPD had been slightly ahead in those constituencies) (Forschungsgruppe Wahlen 1983: 10). Regional differences remained very visible: only one of the CDU–CSU best constituencies was in northern Germany: Cloppenburg-Vechta. All the best constituencies for the SPD were in the Ruhr area.

The 1987 campaign: gains for the smaller parties

The 1987 campaign centred on the record of the coalition. This was regarded favourably by the electorate, who especially approved of the performance of Genscher as Foreign Minister. Economic indicators, such as the strength of the currency and reduction in levels of government debt, allowed Kohl and his cabinet to claim that the 1982 'Wende' had been a success. Land elections had suggested that the Greens were making progress in gaining broader electoral support, though otherwise these elections suggested that the coalition parties (CDU–CSU and FDP) were more popular than the opposition parties. A series of scandals and mishandled situations, ranging from the Flick affair (a series of illegal payments to parties, which hit the FDP especially hard) to the controversial 1985 ceremony in Bitburg military cemetery attended by Kohl and President Reagan, had negative effects on the coalition parties.

The SPD selected the well-respected minister-president of North Rhine-Westphalia, Rau, as the party's new chancellor-candidate For the first time, the Green party had a representative in the now-traditional televised debate near the close of the campaign.

The campaign included a number of themes which the Greens exploited, including the Chernobyl disaster and the pollution of the Rhine by a chemical spillage in Switzerland. Indeed, environmental protection rose from fifth place in the 1983 election to second place (after unemployment) as a priority issue for the electorate (Forschungsgruppe Wahlen 1987: 39). The SPD could not credibly attack the economic record of the government, so promised a more humane version of existing policies. A number of policies, such as attitudes of the government towards countries of the communist bloc, the right of asylum and policies relating to demonstrators, allowed the FDP to profile itself as a liberal corrective to what otherwise might be overly-restrictive policies of the Christian Democrats. The FDP again pursued an explicit policy of seeking list votes from voters inclined to identify with either the CDU–CSU or SPD, but were committed to continuation of the coalition with the Christian Democrats. The SPD was in a dilemma. Rau had excluded any possibility of the SPD governing in coalition with the Greens, yet it was obvious that the SPD would neither have sufficient seats to govern alone nor be able to tempt the FDP to form a coalition with it. The date of the election meant that campaigning was interrupted by the Christmas holidays and that normal patterns of street campaigning were abandoned because of the harsh weather.

Compared to 1983, the Christian Democrats and the SPD declined in terms of vote-share. The CDU–CSU recorded its lowest share of the vote since 1949, but had encouraging results in Hamburg, Hesse and Saarland. The FDP and the Greens both increased their share of the vote. The SPD lost votes to both the Christian Democrats and to the Greens, suggesting a crisis of identity. It did secure a good result in North Rhine-Westphalia, because of Rau's prominence as chancellor-candidate. The FDP secured its best results in Baden-Württemberg, Schleswig-Holstein and Hamburg. Baden-Württemberg and Hamburg were also Länder where the Greens were strong, as was Hesse, where they governed in the Land coalition with the SPD. Turnout (84.3 per cent) was the lowest since 1949, partly because of the high probability that the coalition would again be victorious, partly because the election campaign took place in a very cold January. The level of turnout was not affected by the small number of German voters resident in other countries who could, under a law passed in 1985, vote in Bundestag elections.

The coalition cabinet was quickly re-formed, with no surprises in its composition.

The 1990 campaign: affirmation of reunification

The 1990 election was very special: it was the first election to the Bundestag in the newly reunified Germany, and it took place using a one-off variation of the electoral system, to accommodate the special circumstances in which eastern German parties were participating in the election (see chapter 2). Chancellor Kohl again led the Christian Democrats. Lafontaine was selected as chancellor-candidate of the SPD. Though the events of 1990 overshadowed other issues, the economic situation and developments in the European Community (EC) and Eastern Europe also played a role in the campaign. However, though the election was not a plebiscite on reunification, it was seen by the parties, the mass media and the electorate as a means of affirming support for reunification.

Lafontaine's often trenchant criticisms of the way in which reunification had been hurried through as a process were not well received by the voters.

The campaign involved the western German parties in efforts to find ways of attracting votes in eastern Germany, where electoral competition involved new parties, such as the Party of Democratic Socialism (PDS: successor party to the former ruling SED), Alliance '90 (a miscellaneous alliance in various eastern German Länder of new parties created in 1990) and the DSU (German Social Union: a conservative party with some strength especially in Saxony). The Christian Democrats in particular made considerable progress in utilising electronic mailing in the campaign, both to communicate with voters 'on-line', and to exchange information with local party branches about campaigning.

The result was a resounding victory for the Christian Democrat–Liberal coalition, thanks in part to working-class support for the CDU in eastern Germany, and local support there for leading politicians of western German parties with links to eastern Germany, such as Genscher, the FDP leader and Foreign Minister. The FDP even won a constituency seat – their first since 1957 – in Halle, in eastern Germany, thanks to Genscher's ties to that area. The fact that the CDU won six surplus seats made the government majority even larger. The SPD (33.5 per cent overall, and 35.7 per cent in western Germany) had its worst result since 1957. The PDS, thanks to the special variation of the electoral system utilised in 1990, entered the Bundestag, but the western German Greens, having refused to link up with the eastern German Greens before the election, failed to win enough votes in western Germany to qualify for seats.[6]

For a number of reasons, including the large number of elections during 1990 in which voters in the former GDR had had the opportunity to participate which led to a kind of 'voter fatigue', turnout in the 1990 Bundestag election was the lowest ever (77.8 per cent). The CDU–CSU had its largest shares of the vote among those in the older age categories, and more women than men in both eastern and western Germany supported the Christian Democrats. The Greens did best among voters under thirty-five years of age. The FDP seemed to benefit from the acceptance by voters in both eastern and western Germany that coalition government, rather than single-party rule, was preferable (Forschungsgruppe Wahlen, 1990: 69).

Kohl was able to form a new version of the CDU–CSU and FDP coalition which had governed since the end of 1982, though he was careful to include several ministers from eastern Germany in his cabinet.

The 1994 campaign: Kohl's last hurrah

In 1994 it was clear that economic problems arising from reunification were a major issue for the government. Unemployment, especially in eastern Germany, was high and was increasing annually. Overseas trade was becoming a problem rather than an opportunity for German businesses. Adjustment to the changes which were taking place in the EU was another important issue. Unemployment, the economy and pensions were the themes which most voters regarded as of highest priority in the campaign (Zelle 1996: 63). A number of regional scandals had affected the image of the CDU and CSU. Several ministers-president in the Länder and other prominent politicians had been compelled to resign, including Streibl in Bavaria and Späth in Baden-Württemberg. Krause and de Maizière, ministers from eastern Germany, resigned from the government because of alleged links to the 'Stasi' – the GDR secret police.

Kohl again led the Christian Democrats in the campaign, this time against the new SPD leader, Scharping. The SPD attempted to buttress the relatively unknown image of Scharping by including Schröder (minister-president of Lower Saxony) and Lafontaine (minister-president of Saarland) in TV broadcasts, leaflets and posters. The FDP also had a new leader – Kinkel, the Foreign Minister – but his party was in danger of failing to secure the 5 per cent of votes necessary for Bundestag representation, based on its poor results in Land elections and the EP election. A poster theme reflected this anxiety: 'This time everything's at stake – FDP.' An early version of its electoral manifesto contained an unfortunate reference to the FDP as the 'party of the better-off', which was used by its opponents as a campaign weapon. The Greens, absent from the Bundestag since the 1990 election, but now rid of most of the political influence of the fundamentalist wing of the party, were confident of regaining representation in the Bundestag, following a series of encouraging Land election results. The PDS hoped to adjust successfully to the pre-1990 electoral system requirement that a party must obtain 5 per cent of the votes in the whole of the FRG, or win three constituency seats, and thus obtain list seats. Extreme right-wing party successes in Land elections raised questions about whether one of these parties might garner 5 per cent of the votes, but few regarded this as a serious possibility.

The Christian Democrats relied heavily on the popular image of Kohl. They used a controversial theme – the 'red socks' campaign – to try to link the SPD with the PDS. This followed the agreement of the PDS in Saxony-Anhalt to 'tolerate' the SPD–Green coalition (promising support but without joining the government): the so-called 'Magdeburg model'. For instance, a CDU poster read: 'Into the future – but not wearing red socks', and showed a pair of red socks on a washing line. The FDP also utilised this theme in its campaign: one poster showed Fischer (of the Greens) and Scharping on a couch, but with Gysi (of the PDS) seated on a chair close by. The slogan was: 'This is the threat if you don't vote FDP.' The SPD confronted this issue by claiming it would not form a government if Scharping's election as chancellor depended on PDS votes. Another SPD problem was the coalition question. Since the FDP had excluded the possibility of joining a coalition led by the SPD, that left the SPD with the Greens as the only possible coalition partner – or the unlikely prospect of a 'grand' coalition, which the SPD claimed they would join only if Scharping were to be chancellor. The campaign theme of the SPD was the more modern, youthful image of Scharping, when compared to the older Kohl. The PDS emphasised its democratic credentials by having 'open' lists, which included candidates who were not formally members of the party. Since the PDS almost surely would need to win three or more constituencies to enter the Bundestag (as it was unlikely to secure 5 per cent of list votes), its concentration on a constituency-based strategy meant that it often was in direct competition with the SPD. The PDS did state that it would support a coalition formed by the SPD and Greens if necessary, without expecting to join such a coalition. The Greens had made a firm statement favouring a coalition with the SPD, and were disappointed that the SPD refused to reciprocate by making a pre-election declaration about such a coalition. The Greens feared that the SPD might prefer a 'grand coalition' to linking up with the Greens, and this anxiety was given expression in a Green party poster which implored voters to 'Vote Green against a grand coalition – the second vote is decisive'. In contrast to previous elections, the Greens laid emphasis on its more mediagenic personalities, such as Fischer and Antje Vollmer.

The result was again a victory for the governing coalition: the CDU–CSU (41.5 per cent) declined to its lowest vote-share since 1949, but, with the aid of the FDP (6.9 per cent: also its second-worst result ever) and the benefit of surplus seats, retained an overall majority of just six seats. This was in large measure a victory for Kohl, who was preferred to Scharping as chancellor by a considerable margin (Zelle 1996: 55–8). The SPD gained vote-share (36.4 per cent), but even with the Greens' good result (7.3 per cent) could not claim sufficient seats to form a government. The PDS (4.4 per cent) again entered the Bundestag, thanks to the four constituency seats it won in Berlin, which allowed it to overcome its failure to

secure 5 per cent of list votes. Despite 1994 being a year in which numerous Land, EP and local elections had taken place (hence the term:
'Superwahljahr' applied to it in the media), turnout did improve to 79 per
cent, a slight increase compared to the 1990 turnout.

The Christian Democrats retained a substantial part of the working-
class support which it had attracted in eastern Germany in 1990, though
the SPD made gains among such voters. The FDP in both western and
eastern Germany had its highest vote-share among the self-employed.
The Greens attracted relatively high levels of voting support from civil
servants and white-collar employees. The Christian Democrats and
Greens had higher levels of support from female rather than male voters.
For the SPD there was no significant difference in terms of male or female
voters. The FDP had stronger support from male voters.

The Christian Democrat coalition with the FDP was quickly recon-
structed, with no surprises in terms of its composition or policy programme.

The 1998 campaign: all change, for the first time ever

In the period leading up to the election campaign, the decline in support
for the Christian Democrats and for their coalition allies, the FDP, had
been clearly indicated both by Land elections and opinion polls. The SPD
had high hopes of winning the election, and governing either in alliance
with the Greens or, if necessary, in a 'grand coalition' with the Christian
Democrats. For its designated chancellor-candidate the SPD passed over
the new chairman of the party, Lafontaine (who had not been successful
in 1990 as chancellor-candidate). Instead the party selected Schröder, the
minister-president of Lower Saxony who, earlier in 1998, had demonstrated his electoral magnetism by his sweeping victory in the Land election there. The Greens hoped to be invited to join the government,
though the radical proposals of their more idealistic wing had resulted in
several unpopular proposals, such as large increases in taxes on petrol,
being adopted as part of the party's manifesto for the campaign. The PDS
was seeking to retain membership of the Bundestag – and, depending on
how well the party attracted votes, could well complicate the arithmetic
of coalition negotiations and compel the formation of a 'grand coalition'.
The SPD developed a novel campaign organisation ('Kampa'), modelled
on organisations used in American presidential elections, which emphasised swift responses to campaign developments, negative campaigning

and ripostes to criticisms made by other parties, as well as efficient utilisation of the campaign appearances of leading SPD politicians.

The result was a sweeping victory for the SPD. With the support of the
Greens, the SPD could form a government, despite the PDS winning over
5 per cent of the list votes. The CDU–CSU, under the tired leadership of
Kohl, declined to their worst result since 1949. The FDP, though retaining membership of the Bundestag, was for the second successive election
only the fourth largest party, as the Greens had again overtaken them in
terms of seats. For the FDP, this was the first time since 1969 that it would
not be a party of government.

The SPD had their best results in the northern Länder. CDU–CSU
strength was in Bavaria, Baden-Württemberg and Rhineland-Pfalz.
Baden-Württemberg was the Land in which the FDP achieved its highest
share of the vote. The Greens, as usual, were strongest in Bremen,
Hamburg and Berlin. All those parties were noticeably stronger in western
Germany than in the Länder of the former GDR. The PDS remained predominantly an eastern German party (19.1 per cent, compared to 1.1 per
cent in western Germany). 61 per cent of those voting for the FDP lists
voted for CDU–CSU candidates, and 54 per cent of those voting for the
Green party lists voted for SPD candidates. There were no strong gender
differences in voting behaviour, and only the Greens (with a predominantly youthful electorate) had an age profile of voters that was in any way
remarkable. The Christian Democrats gained above-average shares of the
votes of Catholics and Protestants who attended church regularly, and of
Catholics who attended church intermittently (Forschungsgruppe Wahlen
1998: 18, 29).

A coalition of the SPD and Greens was formed, with Fischer, the most
popular and prominent Green politician, as Foreign Minister. Lafontaine
became Minister of Finance, but after some weeks resigned from that
office and from the party chairmanship, leaving the way clear for
Schröder to assume the leadership of the SPD himself. This election was
therefore the first in which none of the parties in government had participated in the pre-election coalition. Kohl assumed responsibility for the
election débâcle, and resigned as party leader.

The 2002 campaign: a close-run thing

None of the parties represented in the Bundestag could look forward to
the 2002 campaign with any great confidence. The SPD had obviously not

kept its 1998 election promises to revive the economy and, above all, to reduce unemployment significantly. Once again, the party relied upon its campaign organisation, 'Kampa', in a larger and more expensive version than in 1998 (Hogwood 2004: 249–50). The Christian Democrats had suffered from the effects of the party finance scandals which had damaged the reputations of Kohl and a number of other senior figures. The FDP had failed to develop a clear profile during their four years in opposition and had an untried leader, Westerwelle, as their standard-bearer. The Greens had been associated with a number of unpopular policies, and the reputations of Fischer and Trittin, two of their ministers, had both been under scrutiny in the mass media during their period in office. The Greens had lost vote-share at every Land election since joining the government in 1998. The PDS had to campaign without using Gysi as their most prominent politician, because of his links to a scandal and his consequential resignation from his position as Economics Minister in the Berlin government. The PDS also was hampered more than other parties by the reduction in size of the Bundestag (see chapter 2), and revision of constituency boundaries which made it more difficult for the party to win constituency seats, especially in Berlin. The Christian Democrats decided, for the second time, to select a CSU leader as chancellor-candidate: Edmund Stoiber, prime minister of Bavaria (the most successful Land in terms of recent economic development) rather than the CDU leader, Angela Merkel. In the early part of the year, Stoiber and the Christian Democrats managed to reduce and then eliminate the opinion poll lead which the SPD had enjoyed for so long, especially by emphasising the fail-ures of the SPD–Green coalition. Only the severe flooding in the Elbe basin in August reversed the favourable trend for the CDU–CSU. The swift and media-savvy reaction of Schröder, the chancellor, attracted support for the SPD at just the right stage of the campaign. Schröder's insistence late in the campaign that his government would not participate in, nor support, any military action against Iraq was also a populist appeal which undoubtedly won votes for his party. Schröder's greater popularity among voters compared to Stoiber outweighed the view among voters that the Christian Democrats, rather than the SPD, were more competent at dealing with the top issue of the campaign: unemployment, and pos-sessed greater competence in dealing with the economy generally (Forschungsgruppe Wahlen 2002: 34–42).

The FDP campaign was strong on novelty (ranging from an over-ambi-tious target of 18 per cent of the vote to a rather incredible effort to have Westerwelle given the status of a 'chancellor-candidate', from aggressive internet campaigning to adoption of American methods of fund-raising) but was weaker in communicating a strong and unambiguous message to the electorate (Bösch 2002: 13–14). Some ill-advised remarks and actions by a deputy-leader, Möllemann, which were considered by many to be anti-Semitic, proved a handicap to the FDP in the campaign, as did its refusal to commit itself to a coalition with the CDU–CSU ahead of the election. The Greens marked their abandonment of their formal opposition to 'personality politics' in their party by promoting Fischer as their most prominent candidate. His personal popularity among voters, his reputation as Foreign Minister and his charismatic campaign style all benefited the Greens. Neither the PDS (riven by internal wrangling about policy direction and campaign tactics) nor the Hamburg-based right-wing Schill party, made much impact on the campaign.

On election night, the outcome was in doubt for many hours. The SPD and Christian Democrats seemed to have almost exactly the same number of votes (and the final result showed that the SPD enjoyed a lead of only just over 6,000 votes). As it was obvious that the PDS would not be allocated list seats (the party won just two constituency seats), the only feasible coalitions were the SPD–Green coalition or an alliance between the Christian Democrats and the FDP. Because the Greens won eight more seats than the FDP, this – together with four 'surplus seats' won by the SPD compared to only one secured by the CDU – meant that the governing coalition was able to have another term of office, with an overall majority of nine seats. The Greens won their first-ever constituency seat, in Berlin. Turnout was 79.1 per cent.

The SPD was rescued by a considerable increase in its vote-share in eastern Germany (no doubt produced by Schröder's response to the flood disaster), though it lost 4 per cent in western Germany. The FDP also made substantial relative gains in eastern Germany, but only a small increase in vote-share in western Germany. The CDU–CSU gained in western Germany, though most of the additional vote-share was obtained in Bavaria, as a tribute to Stoiber. Christian Democrat gains in eastern Germany were very small. The Greens increased their vote-share in western Germany, adding little to their 1998 vote-share in the new Länder. The SPD obtained its best results in northern Länder, especially Bremen, Lower Saxony and Brandenburg. The CDU–CSU were strongest in Bavaria, Baden-Württemberg and Rhineland-Pfalz. The Greens were strongest in the city-states of Bremen, Hamburg and Berlin, while the FDP did best in North Rhine-Westphalia and Rhineland-Pfalz. The Christian Democrats benefited from their greater appeal to male voters (the SPD continued, as in 1998, to be supported more by women than men), a reversal from the pattern that usually existed in the period prior to reunification. The Christian Democrats' share of the vote increased among older segments of the electorate. The FDP and the Greens both found greater support among younger voters than among those aged forty-five and older. As usual, the CDU–CSU obtained above-average shares of the vote from Catholics, and especially from those who attended church regularly. For the PDS, the future looked bleak, despite its electoral strength in Land elections, where the party had gained vote-share in every election since 1998. Its absence as a party group from the Bundestag not only robbed the PDS of a national platform, but gave the party the reputation ahead of the 2006 Bundestag election of being unlikely to win at least 5 per cent of the vote, and hence a party whose voters might end up wasting their vote.

Notes

1　Erhard was in charge of economic policy in the Economic Council, created by the western occupation powers in June 1947.

2　Though one calculation suggests that the CDU won only three seats which without the pacts it would not have won, at the expense of giving up nine seats which it would have won without the pacts with other parties (Erbe 1960: 86).

3　The Hallstein Doctrine was the guiding principle for the Christian Democrat-led governments concerning their attitude towards the GDR. It stated that the FRG would not have diplomatic relations with any country that gave diplomatic recognition to the GDR (with the exception of the USSR).

4　Ratios for Bundestag elections: *1953*: 0.88 FDP second votes for each first vote *1957*: 1.03; *1961*: 1.06; *1965*: 1.2; *1969*: 1.2; *1972*: 1.75; *1976*: 1.07; *1980*: 1.47; *1983*: 2.5; *1987*: 1.94; *1990*: 1.44; *1994*: 2.09; *1998*: 2.07; *2002*: 1.28.

5　Among supporters of the CDU who were displeased with the choice of Strauss as chancellor-candidate, 16.5 per cent gave their list vote to the FDP. Among those supporters pleased that Strauss had been selected, only 2.8 per cent gave their list vote to the FDP, according to an Allensbach survey (Noelle-Neumann 1983: 587).

6　In eastern Germany Alliance '90/the Greens secured eight seats.

6

Second-order elections

The concept of 'second-order' elections

So far, this book has concentrated on Bundestag elections. Bundestag elections decide the party composition of the Bundestag, and thus the range of potential coalitions which can be formed to govern Germany. However, other elections may have political significance: the election of the federal president; the election of local councils; elections to the EP; and Land elections. Since the election of the federal president is an indirect election, influenced strongly by the outcome of elections to the Bundestag and to Land parliaments which determine the party composition of the Electoral College (*Bundesversammlung*), this topic will not be treated directly in this chapter (see Appendix 4). Local elections and elections to the EP will be dealt with only briefly, since the political significance of such elections is usually rather limited – indeed, so much so that they might better be termed: 'third-order elections'. Elections to Land parliaments, on the other hand, are not only important in the context of the politics of the Land in which they occur; they are also of potentially great significance for national politics, not least because of the possible blocking powers of the Bundesrat in dealing with federal legislation.

'Second-order' elections are usually defined as elections which do not directly affect the composition of the national government nor the passage of national legislation. Thus, in France, both presidential and National Assembly elections are 'first-order' elections, as are elections to the House of Commons in the United Kingdom, and presidential and Congressional elections in the United States. In Germany, Bundestag elections are 'first-order' elections. However, since the Bundesrat is the national legislative chamber representing the Land governments and the party composition of those governments is affected by Land elections, a case could be made to suggest that Land elections should also be regarded as 'first-order' elections (Jeffery and Hough 2001: 79). Nevertheless, not all Land elections have important consequences for the composition of the Bundesrat, either because for a long period the Land is an electoral stronghold for one party or another (such as Bavaria for the CSU, or – until recently – Hamburg for the SPD), or because the Land has few seats and votes in the Bundesrat (Hamburg, Bremen and Saarland, for example). Turnout is usually lower than that for Bundestag elections. Voters use the opportunity to punish the governing coalition (see below) and to vote for small or extreme parties to an extent which does not occur at Bundestag elections. So, on balance, Land elections will be treated as 'second-order' elections for the purposes of this book.

An additional factor in Land and local authority electoral politics is the existence in an increasing number of Länder of the possibility of referendums. In Bavaria and Hesse it is compulsory to put constitutional amendments to the electorate through a referendum. In Bavaria there is also the availability of the initiative, a procedure whereby a group of citizens can place legislative proposals on the ballot paper, to be voted on in the form of a referendum. Such methods of direct democracy complicate, and may to an extent detract from the significance of, Land and local council elections (Ismayr 1997: 437, 438).

Local council elections

Article 28 of the Basic Law requires that local authority areas: the communities (Gemeinde), districts (Landkreise) and metropolitan authorities (Stadtkreise), should have elected councils. However, because of local traditions and the influence of the different zonal occupation regimes after the Second World War and the need for the 'new' Länder to invent democratic local government systems after reunification in 1990, the pattern of local authority representative structures and their election varies from region to region. In most areas now, voters elect both the local council and the mayor. In a few areas, once the voters have elected a council, that council chooses either a single person or a collective leadership group to direct the administration of the local authority. Another pattern provides separate political and administrative leadership, each with formally distinct (but often politically linked) authority. Each Land is responsible for stating in its constitution which pattern of local authority structure will exist in that Land, and for deciding upon the method of election of the council and (if appropriate) the mayor. Election periods vary: Bavaria elects its local councils for six years, for example, and Hesse for four years, but most Länder elect councils for a five-year term. Hesse elects its mayors for a six-year period (since 1993), but in Baden-Württemberg mayors are elected for an eight-year term, for instance. Electoral systems vary, though all include a basis of proportional representation. Some Länder, such as North Rhine-Westphalia, use a 5 per cent barrier at local government level, while other Länder have lower barriers or none at all. Frequently some form of cumulative vote (*kumulieren*) is available, by which voters have, say, three votes which they can distribute among three candidates or give two or three votes to a single candidate. Similarly, panachage (*panaschieren*) is also available in some Länder, by which voters can give votes to particular candidates, even on different party lists, affecting the order on the list in which candidates will be elected. Turnout tends to be lower in local elections than in Land or Bundestag elections, though still considerably higher than in British local authority elections. For example, in the election of the lord mayor of Stuttgart in 2004 turnout was 43.1 per cent for the run-off election. In 2004 turnout in local elections in Mecklenburg-Vorpommern was 45.5 per cent; in North Rhine-Westphalia 54.5 per cent; in Rhineland-Pfalz 57.6 per cent; in Saxony-Anhalt 42.2 per cent; in Saxony 46.1 per cent; and in Saarland 56 per cent.

Such local elections have resonance beyond the Land in which they occur for at least three important reasons. First, they serve as a barometer for parties nationally, which is the more important because the Bundestag lacks bye-elections as indicators of changing party popularity. So a good or a poor performance by a party in, say, Thuringia local elections can be compared to the most recent Land election results there and to the performance of the parties in that Land in the previous Bundestag election. Second, local elections can serve as a springboard for small parties, especially as in some Länder seats can be won with fewer than 5 per cent of the vote (Harrison 2000). 'Independent' groups present candidates, sometimes successfully, such as the Association of Independent Voters – Freie Wählergemeinschaft – and other parties compete, parties which rarely, if ever, present candidates outside that Land. Parties such as the PDS, the Greens and extreme right-wing parties may more easily win seats and even mayoral positions in small communities.[1] This provides them with organisational and electoral resources for elections at Land or national level, and offers them opportunities to develop a political reputation in the area. Third, local authorities are less sensitive politically in relation to political experiments, especially in terms of coalitions or political co-operation. Unusual alliances can thus take place at local level, without in any way committing those parties to co-operation in Land or national politics. For instance, there have been cases of local co-operation between the CDU and Greens in North Rhine-Westphalia, and in 2004 the CDU candidate for lord mayor of Stuttgart won a run-off election against an SPD opponent with the explicit support of the Green party candidate, in return for concessions on environmental projects (*Das Parlament* 1 November 2004).

National patterns of party competition, party identification and national or Land-level political issues play a considerable part in explaining electoral behaviour in local elections, in different degrees in different Länder (Eith 1998). Nevertheless, local elections are often strongly affected by local issues, the local performance of parties in control of councils and the reputation of individual politicians, especially the mayors. So, for example, in the local elections in North Rhine-Westphalia on 26 September 2004, an Infratest survey found that 51 per cent of respondents stated that local political issues and performance had determined their voting decision, compared to 33 per cent who claimed that national policy had been decisive, and 15 per cent who stated that Land politics had been the determining factor (*Das Parlament* 4/11 October 2004).

Elections to the EP

Since 1979 the EP has been elected directly in the member states. Elections take place every five years. In the FRG, parties may choose to present a unified national list, or separate Land lists. Each voter has a single vote, to give to a party list. Seats are then allocated proportionally to all parties securing at least 5 per cent of the votes nationally. Turnout has been lower than at Bundestag or Land parliament elections, and has been declining in recent elections (as it has in most of the member-states). In 2004 turnout was 43 per cent. Even this low level of turnout was artificially boosted by the fact that in seven of the sixteen Länder local council or Land elections were taking place simultaneously. In those Länder turnout was 51.3 per cent. In the other nine Länder, turnout was only 39 per cent on average (Forschungsgruppe Wahlen 2004a: 11).

The development of EU-wide party organisations (alliances of similar parties in various member-states) has occurred in recent years, and, once elected, German parties operate in cross-national party alliances in the EP. Despite these cross-national party institutions and the costly efforts made by EU institutions and other groups to promote European integration and to emphasise the significance of the EP, voters in Germany, as in the United Kingdom and elsewhere in the EU, are hard to persuade that these elections should be about European issues. 'Taking into account the structure of the electoral campaign as well as the voters' own perceptions, the recent German elections to the European Parliament were clearly national rather than European in character' was the judgement of one expert (Helms 1999: 165). This assessment was confirmed by comments by a leading research institute in 1999 that the European elections were seen as a verdict on the SPD–Green government (Forschungsgruppe Wahlen 1999: 60).[2] This comment could be applied also to the 2004 elections: a survey in February 2004 for the Politbarometer of Forschungsgruppe Wahlen found that 47 per cent of voters were 'interested' or 'very interested' in politics, but only 22 per cent showed the same levels of interest in European politics (Roth and Kornelius 2004: 46). The parties themselves often emphasise national, rather than European, issues in their campaigns. Relatively little attention is given to EP elections by the media. Consequently the minority of voters who do go to the polling stations tend to cast their votes on the basis of domestic, rather than European, considerations, and the parties themselves assess the results at least partly in terms of national popularity. This can give rise to protest voting (the success of the extreme right-wing Republican party in winning seats in 1989 is an example), and can allow parties such as the Association of Free Citizens (*Bund freier Bürger*) to have a platform for their cause.[3] Because of the unavailability of split-voting (each voter has a single vote, for a party list), the FDP and the Greens sometimes fail to obtain the levels of support which they might in a Bundestag election.

Land electoral systems and electoral behaviour

In general, the electoral systems used for Land elections are broadly similar to that used for electing the Bundestag (see chapter 2). All the systems are based on proportional representation, usually with a form of compensation for parties which otherwise would be disadvantaged by the existence of surplus seats (a compensation which does not exist in Bundestag elections). For example, in the Lower Saxony Land election in 2003, the CDU gained fourteen surplus seats, so the SPD was given ten compensatory seats, and the FDP and Green party each two such seats. Two somewhat exceptional cases stand out: Baden-Württemberg and Bavaria, and these will be described more fully. The other fourteen Länder use some variant of list-based systems, usually involving an element of constituency-based election and often using two differentiated votes, though five Länder use a single vote (including Baden-Württemberg, and Hamburg until the proposed new electoral system takes effect). The trend towards five-year terms has been noticeable in recent years, so that in 2004 only five of the sixteen Länder still had four-year terms.

The electoral system used in Baden-Württemberg is unusual in that it is based on a single vote cast in seventy constituencies of very unequal sizes. There are no formal party lists. Since a constitutional amendment in February 1995, the Baden-Württemberg parliament is elected for a five-year term. The Land is divided into four administrative regions (Regierungsbezirke), each containing between eleven and twenty-six constituencies. In each constituency, the candidate with the most votes wins the seat. To provide proportional representation, within each administrative region parties win additional seats according to their overall share of the vote in that administrative region (taking account of any constituency seats which they have already won), provided they have obtained at least 5 per cent of the votes in the Land as a whole. These additional seats – at least fifty in the Land as a whole – are awarded to the 'best' losing candidates of each party. However, 'best' is calculated on the basis of *total* votes won, not *percentage* of votes. So a candidate of, say, the FDP who won 20 per cent of the vote and came third in a small constituency may fail to be awarded a seat, but an FDP candidate with 12 per cent in fourth place in a larger constituency may be given a seat because the 12 per cent in that constituency represents more votes in aggregate than the 20 per cent of the unsuccessful colleague. Should a party win more constituency seats in an administrative region than the total proportional allocation of seats in that administrative region for that party, it retains such surplus seats, but other parties are awarded compensatory seats in sufficient numbers to preserve proportionality, if necessary. So the CDU in 2001 with 44.8 per cent of the vote won sixty-three constituency seats, including six surplus seats. The SPD (33.3 per cent of the vote) obtained two additional seats in compensation. However, as surplus seats and compensatory seats are allotted on a regional, and not a Land, basis, this procedure has been criticised and certainly can add considerably and unnecessarily to the size of the Land parliament, which has varied between 120 seats (the minimum) in 1956, 1964 and 1972, and 155 seats

in 1996 (Trefs 2003: 88, 100–3).[4] An odd effect of this system is that a constituency may have not one, but two or three elected MdLs (Members of
the Landtag), especially if it has a large electorate.[5] A medium-size constituency could have two elected MdLs: the winner, and a third-place candidate from, say, the Greens, but not the second-placed losing SPD
candidate. The absence of a list means that parties cannot so easily control
the allocation of safe seats: there is a degree of uncertainty concerning
which of its candidates (especially 'losing' candidates) will be elected.

The Bavarian electoral system has undergone a number of changes of
detail since the first post-war Land election in December 1946, particularly concerning the number of seats and the qualifying percentage necessary to obtain representation in the Land parliament.[6] The Land is
divided into seven electoral regions based on the seven Regierungsbezirke
(administrative regions). There are 180 seats available: ninety-two from
single-member constituencies and eighty-eight from party lists in the
electoral regions. Each voter has two votes (on separate ballot papers):
one for a constituency candidate, and one for the regional list. However,
unlike other two-vote systems in Germany, the voter can use the second
(list) vote for a particular candidate on the list, in this way helping a lowly-
placed candidate to move up the order and thus perhaps gain a list seat.
This is used sufficiently frequently to produce some unexpected results,
with popular or well-known candidates securing seats where their origi-
nal list placement would have suggested that they would be unsuccessful.[7]
Candidates can stand in a constituency as well as on the list. Where the
constituency candidate is also a list candidate, voters cannot in that constituency also vote for that person on the list. Votes for list candidates
consist of those received on the list itself plus, if applicable, those received
by that candidate in a constituency, so there is a benefit to be gained from
contesting a constituency, even if unsuccessfully. For example, in 1998
Ursula Männle, a minister in the Land government and selected in third
place on the CSU list, did not contest a constituency and it was only by
good fortune that she managed to win a seat at the Land election that year.
Her list vote alone, high though it was, placed her on the very margin of
those elected from the CSU list in Oberbayern. In contrast, Hildegard
Kronawitter, selected as sixteenth on the SPD Oberbayern list, actually
came second on her party's list because of a large personal list vote, twice
as many as the third-placed candidate, which was supplemented by a considerable constituency vote. As in Baden-Württemberg, since 1974 compensatory seats can be allotted if surplus seats distort proportionality.
Another unusual feature of the Bavarian electoral system is that, unlike

elections to the Bundestag or in other Länder using a mixed-member system similar to that used for the Bundestag, a candidate winning a constituency whose party fails to qualify for seats under the 5 per cent rule is not allowed to take the seat: the second-placed candidate is declared elected instead (an eventuality extremely unlikely to occur, of course).

The other fourteen Länder use a system similar to that employed for Bundestag elections, with relatively minor differences. Thanks largely to pressure from the FDP, especially when that party has been in coalition, several Länder have moved from a single-vote to a double-vote system (which benefits the FDP and perhaps other small parties by allowing split-voting, see chapter 2).[8] Only Baden-Württemberg, Bremen, Hamburg, North Rhine-Westphalia and Saarland still use a single-vote system. Of these, Bremen, Hamburg and the Saarland employ party lists only, not constituencies, though Hamburg is likely to adopt a completely different system for its 2008 Land election.[9] The smallest Land, Bremen, is an oddity in that its two non-contiguous cities, Bremen itself and Bremerhaven, are separate electoral districts. Until 2003, Bremen elected eighty legislators, Bremerhaven twenty. The number of seats was then reduced to eighty-three, with Bremen electing sixty-seven and Bremerhaven sixteen. The qualification is also separate: 5 per cent in either city will qualify a party for an allocation of seats in that city, even if overall the party secures under 5 per cent. This benefited the extreme right-wing DVU party in 1987, 1999 and 2003. Contesting the 1987 election as 'List D', it obtained 5.4 per cent in Bremerhaven (though only 3.4 per cent in the Land as a whole), and in 1999 won 6 per cent in Bremerhaven (only 3 per cent in the Land as a whole), and thus in each case qualified for one seat. In 2003 the DVU won 7.1 per cent in Bremerhaven (2.3 per cent overall), and so was awarded one seat, as was the FDP (5.7 per cent in Bremerhaven, 4.2 per cent overall).

The standard size of each Land legislature (i.e. before any surplus and compensatory seats are included) varies from 201 in North Rhine-Westphalia to fifty-one in Saarland, though the variation is not always a reflection of population size. The Land parliament of Hesse, for example, has 110 seats, and that of Baden-Württemberg 120, whereas the much smaller Land of Hamburg has 121 seats. Where mixed-member systems are used, the ratio between constituency and list seats varies from equality (e.g. in Brandenburg, Saxony and Thuringia) to a 3:1 ratio in North Rhine-Westphalia. Another source of variation is the method employed to allocate seats among the parties: some Länder still use the d'Hondt method (employed in Bundestag elections until the 1987 election); others have adopted the Hare–Niemeyer formula, as now used in Bundestag elections (see Appendix 6).

Electoral behaviour in Land elections can vary significantly from that in Bundestag elections. Turnout is lower, though still relatively high for second-order elections. In February 2003, for example, turnout in the Hesse Land election was 64.6 per cent and on the same day in Lower Saxony it was 67 per cent. In May in Bremen it was 61.4 per cent. In September in Bavaria the turnout of 57.3 per cent was the second lowest ever at a Land election in post-war western Germany (Forschungsgruppe Wahlen 2003: 22). In 2004 turnout in Hamburg was 68.7 per cent. In the 'new' Länder in eastern Germany turnout is below that in western Germany, as is the case in Bundestag elections.[10] In Saxony-Anhalt in 2002 it was only 56.5 per cent and in Thuringia in 2004 turnout was only 54 per cent, for instance.[11]

It does seem that voters are more volatile in Land elections than in Bundestag elections, as measured, for example, by the swings between parties at any two successive Land elections. For instance, in Berlin in 2001 the CDU lost 17 per cent and in Saxony-Anhalt in 2002 it gained over 15 per cent of vote share. It lost 7 per cent in Brandenburg in 2004. In Hamburg in 2004 the CDU nearly doubled its previous vote-share: it increased from 26.2 per cent to 47.2 per cent. The SPD in 1999 lost nearly 15 per cent in Brandenburg and 11 per cent in Thuringia, over 15 per cent in Saxony-Anhalt in 2002, 9 per cent in Bavaria in 2003 and 7 per cent in Brandenburg in 2004. Voters are more ready to support small or even extreme parties, and are certainly willing to deliver a judgement on the federal government. So extreme right-wing parties such as the NPD (in the 1960s and in 2004 in Saxony), the DVU (in Bremen, Schleswig-Holstein, Saxony-Anhalt and Brandenburg) and Republicans (in Baden-Württemberg in the 1990s) have all had, often unanticipated, successes in Land elections. Rarely, though, has such a party been successful in retaining representation in a Land parliament (the Republicans in Baden-Württemberg in 1992 and 1996 and the DVU in Brandenburg in 1999 and 2004 being exceptional cases). The successes of the STATT party in 1993 and the Schill party in 2001 in Hamburg were newsworthy at the time, but in both cases attempts to develop the parties beyond the confines of Hamburg came to nothing, and neither in Bundestag elections nor in the next Land election did these parties have success. Another such case was 'Arbeit für Bremen', which won seats in 1995, but not at the next Land election in 1999. Land elections certainly helped the Greens to establish themselves. Local Green parties won seats in Bremen and Baden-

Württemberg in 1979 and 1980 and, though the party failed to win Bundestag seats in 1980, further Land election successes in Hamburg and Hesse gave it impetus and encouragement so that it won seats in the Bundestag in 1983. The PDS has been helped by its successes in Land elections in eastern Germany, where in 2004 it was the second largest party in every Land except Mecklenburg-Vorpommern, and indeed the largest party in East Berlin (larger there than the SPD and CDU together) (Jesse 2004). The PDS has even been in governing coalitions with the SPD (in Berlin and Mecklenburg-Vorpommern). These Land election successes have not tailed off in line with the performance of the PDS in Bundestag elections: they have increased their vote-share in every eastern German Land except Mecklenburg-Vorpommern. For the Greens and the FDP, representation in Land parliaments and even participation in Land coalitions in periods when national support for those parties has been dangerously close to the crucial 5 per cent boundary has boosted the morale of party supporters, provided the parties with publicity and organisational resources, and allowed them in Bundestag campaigns to point to their credibility as participants in Land politics. However, the situation can be reversed. The FDP has managed to overcome the effects of a series of poor Land election results (in 1994, for example) and in Bundestag elections still obtains over 5 per cent of the national vote. The Greens experienced a series of Land elections reaching back four years to 1998 in which the party always lost vote-share, and sometimes Land parliamentary representation, yet the party won 8.6 per cent in the Bundestag election in 2002. For both the FDP and the Greens participation in coalitions in national government accounted for some of their better performance in Bundestag elections than in earlier Land elections. Equally, in Länder where these parties have been in coalitions, or were likely to be required to provide the CDU or SPD with a governing majority, they have tended to do better than expected in Land elections.

The relative strengths of parties in the Länder can vary, and it is often the case that the larger parties have long periods of dominance in particular Länder. The CSU has long been a dominant party in Bavarian politics. It has secured over 50 per cent of the vote in Land elections since 1970. The SPD enjoyed long periods of dominance in Hamburg, Bremen and Berlin and, more recently, in Saarland and North Rhine-Westphalia. The CDU has been dominant for long periods in Hesse, Baden-Württemberg, Rhineland-Pfalz, Schleswig-Holstein and Saarland, and appears since reunification to have developed a dominant position in Saxony. However, as in national politics, so in Land politics party systems can change, and periods of dominance come to an end (Roberts 1990: 101–4).

Land elections and federal politics

Land elections play a dual role: they are clearly concerned with Land political issues and affect the composition of the future government of the Land, but also they have inescapable links to national politics. The impact of the CDU–CSU petition campaign against the Schröder government's proposals to permit dual nationality in the 1999 Hesse Land election is just one example of a national political issue influencing the outcome of a Land election. In Land elections in Saarland, Saxony and Brandenburg in September 2004 prominent federal politicians (such as Laurenz Meyer, then CDU General-Secretary) as well as Land politicians laid the blame for poor results for the Christian Democrats and SPD on their support for necessary reforms to the welfare system, and especially proposals ('Hartz IV') to adjust employment policies in order that the FRG could more effectively compete against their economic rivals. Surveys found that in both Brandenburg and Saxony unemployment was far and away the most important issue for voters (87 per cent mentioned that issue in each Land), with education (12 per cent in Saxony and 11 per cent in Brandenburg) and Hartz IV (9 per cent in Saxony and 11 per cent in Brandenburg) as the next-ranked issues (Forschungsgruppe Wahlen 2004c: 32; Forschungsgruppe Wahlen 2004d: 32). A problem in differentiating federal and Land political effects is that, in a growing number of policy areas, competence is shared between the two levels of government: environmental protection, aspects of economic policy and education are examples.

There is no serious case made that Land elections are solely concerned with national political issues or other effects on national politics. In each Land election there will be local issues that play an important role: crime in Hamburg, regional unemployment in Saxony-Anhalt, Brandenburg, Hesse and Lower Saxony, the size of the city's debt in Berlin and education in Baden-Württemberg have all been among dominant themes in recent Land elections. The popularity of Land parties and of Land party leaders can also be important. Surveys show that voters may have different evaluations of Land parties and leaders than they have of those parties and their leaders at national level. For example, the unexpected triumph of the CDU leading candidate, Ole von Beust, in the Hamburg Land election in

February 2004 was attributed to his personal popularity rather than to the popularity of his party in national politics. On a scale of + 5 to − 5, the CDU in Hamburg was rated by respondents at + 1.2, but the CDU national party rated at only + 0.4. The rating for von Beust was + 2.0, while that for Mirow, his SPD rival, was only + 0.7 (Forschungsgruppe Wahlen 2004b: 23–4, 29). The contrast between the CDU vote-share in that Land election (47.2 per cent) and the CDU performance in Hamburg in the 2002 Bundestag election (28.1 per cent) reflects this situation also. The differences between electoral behaviour in a Land election and in the Bundestag election in that same Land (even in some cases when a Land election is held on the same day as a Bundestag election, or within a few weeks of such an election) underline this degree of autonomy of Land elections. The availability of parties as coalition partners for each other in a Land government may also diverge from the pattern of availability at that particular time at federal level.

However, it is also obvious that Land elections, to varying degrees, have an impact upon national politics, in several ways.

First, Land elections that result in changes or modifications of Land governments affect the balance of votes in the Bundesrat, the second chamber of the federal legislature. The Bundesrat has quite wide powers of veto (see Appendix 7). Because Länder have different numbers of votes in the Bundesrat (some have six, others between three and five), a change of government in a large Land such as North Rhine-Westphalia can produce large swings in the voting strength of the parties in the Bundesrat, and can lead to the opposition possessing a blocking two-thirds majority in that chamber, which means that the coalition can pass only legislation to which the opposition consents. The opposition to the federal government has possessed a majority in the Bundesrat in thirty-two of the fifty-five years of the existence of the FRG (as at the end of 2004) (Patzelt 2004: 272). In autumn 2004, following Land elections in September, the SPD–Green party coalition could normally count on the votes of only four Länder (a total of seventeen votes), while the opposition Christian Democrats and FDP could rely on thirty-seven votes from eight Länder. There were four Länder: Brandenburg; Bremen; Rhineland-Pfalz; Saxony) where the existence of a 'grand' coalition or other 'incongruent' coalition meant that fifteen Land votes were generally neutralised. By capturing in further Land elections just nine votes the Christian Democrats would obtain a blocking two-thirds majority, by controlling forty-six of the sixty-nine votes. The Kohl government similarly had to confront a 'hostile' Bundesrat in its closing years, which hampered Kohl's efforts to introduce reforms. Of course, sometimes Länder or regional interests complicate the arithmetic: eastern Länder may sometimes vote together irrespective of party loyalties, for example. Incongruent coalitions (such as a 'grand' coalition) may neutralise opposition votes at times. But the real threat of creation of a blocking majority does sometimes imbue a Land election with a political significance over and above its normal importance. Even if the opposition does not have a majority in the Bundesrat, Land election results can change the relative power of small parties. When the SPD was defeated in the Hesse Land election in 1999, that gave Mecklenburg-Vorpommern increased importance, since the SPD governed in that Land with the PDS as its coalition partner and needed the votes of that Land more than before. The PDS therefore had increased influence *vis-à-vis* the SPD in consequence.

Land elections also sometimes affect the future pattern of coalitions at federal level. Before the 1960s, Land coalitions quite often consisted of pairings or larger combinations of parties which were not always congruent with the coalition governing in Bonn, including 'grand coalitions' and all-party governments. In Baden-Württemberg for a short period in 1952 Reinhold Maier, the FDP Land party leader, led a coalition of the FDP, SPD and the refugee party (GB–BHE), much to the dismay of the more right-wing FDP leadership in Bonn and the CDU–CSU, the FDP's coalition partner in the federal government. However, this was not regarded as any form of precedent for a coalition between the SPD and FDP at national level (or indeed in other Länder). Nor was the creation of a multi-party government (including the FDP) under an SPD minister-president, in Bavaria (1954–57) intended as a signal about coalition at national levels. The decision by the FDP, taken precisely in order to 'blackmail' the CDU–CSU, by switching sides in North Rhine-Westphalia in 1956 (the 'Young Turks' Revolt') and joining a coalition government led by the SPD, had no real significance for coalition options at national level, though it contributed to the decision in 1957 not to state a coalition preference in advance of the Bundestag election. Perhaps more influential as a forerunner of a likely coalition at national level between the SPD and FDP were coalition governments between those two parties in Bremen from 1959 until 1971, and in Lower Saxony (1959–67). In 1966, following the collapse of the federal coalition after the refusal of the FDP to accept the financial policies of Erhard and the CDU–CSU, the formation of a coalition in North Rhine-Westphalia between the SPD and FDP came as a warning to the Christian Democrats that in future they could no longer count automatically on the FDP to be their coalition partner in the

Bonn government. The FDP then entered a coalition with the SPD in Bonn after the 1969 election. 'Incongruent' Land coalitions between the CDU and FDP in Lower Saxony and the Saarland (both formed in 1977) during the lifetime of the SPD–FDP coalition in Bonn prepared the way for the decision by the FDP to pair up with Kohl's Christian Democrats in government following the constructive vote of no confidence in 1982. The Land election in Hesse in September 1982 was seen as a final opportunity to test the viability of the FDP entering a national coalition with the Christian Democrats (though the FDP did not secure 5 per cent in that Land election, so a new coalition could not be formed in Hesse). Ahead of the 1975 Land election in Rhineland-Pfalz (where Kohl was minister-president) the FDP was ready to enter a coalition with the CDU, even though it was in coalition with the SPD in Bonn, thanks to the 'bridge-building' with the FDP which Kohl and the Land CDU had fostered after the SPD–FDP coalition had been formed in 1969 (Kohl 1988: 474–5). However, this option was not in the end required. The FDP kept its coalition options open even when acting as a loyal coalition partner to the CDU–CSU in Bonn, by entering coalitions led by the SPD in Hamburg in 1987 and in Rhineland-Pfalz in 1991. The formation of a federal coalition between the SPD and the Greens in 1998 was unsurprising, given that these two parties had already formed governing coalitions with some political success in several Länder, including Hamburg, Hesse and North Rhine-Westphalia. In Mecklenburg-Vorpommern, a coalition between the SPD and PDS constructed in 1998 remained in office following the Land election in 2002. The existence of that coalition (as well as the controversial coalition between these two parties formed in Berlin in 2001) might have affected the uncompromising stance of the SPD party leadership concerning the impossibility of having the PDS in government at national level, had the SPD and Greens lacked an overall majority after the 2002 Bundestag election. Of course, Land elections can provide a retrospective verdict on coalition changes at national level. The FDP was punished in Land elections after its decisions in 1969 to enter a coalition for the first time ever with the SPD. Indeed, three very poor results in Land elections in North Rhine-Westphalia, the Saarland and Lower Saxony in 1970 encouraged potential defectors from the FDP parliamentary party, disaffected because of the coalition with the SPD, to cross to join the Christian Democrat parliamentary group. Then in 1982–83 the FDP again experienced disappointing Land election results after its abandonment of its coalition with the SPD and its alliance with the Christian Democrats (see chapter 5).

Another effect which Land elections may have on national politics is by showcasing Land politicians. A relatively recent case of a Land election producing a chancellor was the victory of Schröder in the Lower Saxony Land election in March 1998, where he was able to retain his post as minister-president, but which confirmed that he should be the chancellor-candidate of the SPD to challenge Kohl in the Bundestag election in September of that year. Success in Land elections has been a principal factor in the selection of a large majority of chancellors or chancellor-candidates. Brandt in Berlin, Kiesinger in Baden-Württemberg and Kohl in Rhineland-Pfalz all headed governments at Land level prior to becoming chancellor. The four unsuccessful SPD chancellor-candidates who preceded Schröder: Vogel (Berlin), Rau (North Rhine-Westphalia), Lafontaine (Saarland) and Scharping (Rhineland-Pfalz) had all been prominent in Land politics. The unsuccessful Christian Democrat chancellor-candidate in 2002, Stoiber, was minister-president of Bavaria. At a less prominent level, Land politicians may parlay their local successes into appointment at ministerial level in the federal government. Eichel and Fischer (Hesse), Clement (North Rhine-Westphalia) and Stolpe (Brandenburg) in the 2002 SPD–Green coalition government are recent examples.[12] Of course, the transfer process works the other way as well. Examples include Lübke, the second federal president, who gave up his seat in the Bundestag in 1950 to become Agriculture Minister in the North Rhine-Westphalia Land government; Meyers and Kiesinger, both elected for the CDU in 1957, left the Bundestag in 1958 and 1959, respectively, to become ministers-president of North Rhine-Westphalia and Baden-Württemberg; Börner, elected in 1972, resigned from the Bundestag in 1976 to become minister-president of Hesse.

Land elections offer small parties the opportunity to obtain electoral successes which they then can hope to extend to Bundestag elections. In the period of the grand coalition (1966–69) the NPD gained representation in Baden-Württemberg, Bavaria, Bremen, Hesse, Lower Saxony, Rhineland-Pfalz and Schleswig-Holstein, often with well over the requisite 5 per cent share of the vote. So when the 1969 Bundestag election took place, many observers predicted that the NPD would obtain seats, but its 4.3 per cent vote-share was insufficient. The party then rapidly faded away, losing its representation in all the Land parliaments where it had previously won seats. More recently, successes by other extreme right-wing parties, especially the Republicans (which won seats in two successive elections in Baden-Württemberg), the NPD (Saxony) and the DVU (successes in Brandenburg, Bremen, Schleswig-Holstein and Saxony-

Anhalt) have raised concerns about these parties winning Bundestag seats in the next election. Neither the STATT party nor the Schill party, which won seats in Hamburg elections, managed either to replicate such successes in other Länder, or win Bundestag seats. Indeed, both were 'one-election wonders'. The Green party, on the other hand, did translate Land election successes into Bundestag representation in 1983, and its role in Land coalitions such as Hesse made it a credible coalition partner for the SPD in the federal government in 1998. There is a similarity in this respect between Land elections and bye-elections in the United Kingdom, where smaller parties can concentrate resources, including campaigning by prominent nationally known politicians, in a way that would not be possible for them in nation-wide elections.

Finally, in a political system which lacks bye-elections (since vacant seats in the Bundestag are filled from the lists of the party whose MdB has vacated the seat), Land elections serve as interim tests of the popularity of the government and the opposition parties. Even in the 1950s, politicians tried to make Land elections into plebiscites on national politics (Pollmann 1997: 242). Though politicians (especially those whose party has not done well) are anxious to emphasise that Land election results cannot be taken directly as indicators of national popularity, nevertheless they do often serve as warnings of significant changes in support for parties and as pointers to the outcome of the next Bundestag election, especially if they occur within a year of that election. Trends in such elections often confirm the monthly opinion surveys of the major research institutes. The poor results for the SPD in Land elections after the Bundestag election of September 2002, especially in Hesse, Lower Saxony, Saxony-Anhalt and Hamburg, were in line with the levels of support shown in such surveys. The election outcomes, as well as the research available to the parties during and after the election campaign, can alert party leaders to problems which they have to confront, or issues which they need to address. The success of the Schill party in Hamburg brought forcefully to the attention of other parties the importance of the 'law-and-order' issue for Hamburg voters. The failure of the PDS to 'break through' in Land elections in western Germany presaged the lack of progress made by that party in the Bundestag elections in 2002 (McKay 2004a: 61–7). Unusually high voting support for extreme right-wing parties is seen less as a dangerous drift of voters to the extremes of the political spectrum, more as a level of protest voting to which establishment parties then need to respond.

However, Land election results are not always a useful predictor of the likely outcome of a Bundestag election. Not only is the context of the

Bundestag election different from those of Land elections; since turnout is lower in Land elections, there are additional voters in Bundestag elections whose party preferences may well not match those of voters who voted in Land elections. The successes of the SPD and Greens in the 1998 Bundestag election were not in line with Land election results. The SPD lost vote-share in nine of the eleven elections which took place after the Bundestag election of 1994 and before that of 1998 (not including those simultaneous with Bundestag election), yet in the Bundestag election in 1998 it gained 4.5 per cent. The CDU gained vote-share in seven of those eleven elections, yet its Bundestag election result showed a decrease of 5.8 per cent compared to 1994. The Greens gained vote-share in all but the final three of the eleven Land elections, yet its Bundestag election vote-share declined by 0.6 per cent.

As with mid-term Congressional elections in the United States, which are expected normally to go against the party in the White House at the time, so there is an expectation that Land elections will tend to benefit parties not in the federal government coalition. In an important research article, Dinkel analysed all Land elections between 1949 and 1972. He compared the Land election result for the governing parties at federal level with the results in that Land for those parties in the Bundestag elections immediately before and immediately after the Land election. A coalition which received in a Land 50 per cent in the Bundestag election in, say, 1961 and 54 per cent in the same Land in 1965 should expect, on a 'trend line', 52 per cent in a Land election midway between those Bundestag elections. He found that in sixty-five of sixty-seven cases, the coalition parties received a vote-share below the trend line. On average, the coalition parties received only 88.3 per cent of the 'expected' vote. This, claimed Dinkel, showed that there was a relationship between voting in Land elections and the popularity of the federal governing coalition, since otherwise the actual vote for coalition parties would be randomly distributed above and below the 'expected' vote trend line (Dinkel 1977: 349). Jeffery and Hough used the Dinkel model to examine how well it fitted results since the period to which Dinkel applied it. They found that in 101 out of 103 cases of Land elections up to 1990, federal coalition parties had Land results below the 'trend line'. The main opposition party did slightly better than its expected vote, and small parties did much better. Lower turnout in Land elections is a phenomenon that has to be taken into account in explaining this periodic cycle of voting in Land elections, as must factors such as the congruence between the incumbent coalition in the Land and the federal coalition, and the distance in time between the Land election and the previous or forthcoming Bundestag election. The period 1990–98 seemed to confirm the effects identified by Dinkel and by Jeffery and Hough for the 'old' FRG, though the data set for post-reunification Germany up to 1998 was rather small (Jeffery and Hough 2001: 80–9).[13]

Do second-order elections matter?

Clearly, they do: especially Land elections. They matter for their own sake. Take the case of local council elections. Local communities are responsible for policies which directly affect the day-to-day lives of citizens, and though those policies may not be as closely identifiable with national party ideologies and programmes as are policies in Land or Bundestag elections, it may well make a large difference locally which parties (and which politicians) win votes and hence seats. The EP elections are the least significant for their own sake, even though that Parliament has acquired increased competencies since the 1990s, shown by its refusal to accept certain new Commissioners in 2004. Land governments have responsibility in the German federal system for a range of highly significant policy sectors: transport, education, aspects of environmental safety, policing and the judicial system among them. These elections matter also because they are interwoven with other political arenas. In particular, Land elections can have an impact on the federal government and federal legislation through changes in party voting strength in the Bundesrat. Whether the application of the label 'second-order' elections is fully justified or not, such elections are of great political importance.

Notes

1 The PDS has over 100 seats in local councils in the western Länder, and has had particularly good results in certain towns in western Germany such as Duisburg, Göttingen and Oldenburg (McKay 2004a: 60–1). In Konstanz, in Baden-Württemberg, Horst Frank, the first Green party lord mayor in Germany, was elected for a second eight-year term in July 2004 (*Frankfurter Rundschau* 27 July 2004).
2 A survey by Forschungsgruppe Wahlen found that in 1999 59 per cent of voters claimed that national politics dominated in their decision how to vote in the EP elections; only 34 per cent claimed that European politics dominated in their decision (Roth and Kornelius 2004: 49, 52). In 2004 51 per cent mentioned

federal politics as determining their decision how to vote, and only 43 per cent mentioned European politics as determining that decision. This was confirmed by respondents claiming that unemployment (70 per cent) the economy (20 per cent), health (11 per cent) and pensions (10 per cent) were the most important issues in the election. Voters perceived decisions made by the EP as less important than those made by the Bundestag, Land legislature or local councils (Forschungsgruppe Wahlen, 2004a: 28–9, 32)

3 The Association of Free Citizens (Bund freier Bürger – BfB) was formed in 1994 by Manfred Brunner (a former Commissioner in the EC) and his associates, to gain support for a more critical attitude in Germany concerning the Maastricht Treaty and progress towards monetary union. It failed to obtain a ruling from the Constitutional Court to prevent the FRG from, as the party saw it, surrendering constitutional and democratic principles under the Maastricht Treaty. The party supported free market principles, and wanted a plebiscitary element in the Basic Law. In the 1994 elections for the EP it obtained only 1.1 per cent, and faded away after failing to make any impact in Land elections.

4 The number of seats in fact has not exceeded 128 (2001) except for the two elections in 1992 and 1996, when the Republican party gained a significant percentage of the vote and won seats in the Land parliament. In those two elections so many surplus and compensatory seats were needed that the Land parliament had 146 and 155 seats, respectively. For example, in 1996 the CDU won eighteen surplus seats, but the SPD was awarded eight compensatory seats, the Greens four, the Republicans three and the FDP two.

5 In the 1996 Land election, of the seventy constituencies, twenty-one elected only one MdL, twenty-six elected two; twelve had three; nine had four; and two (Nürtingen and Enz) had five (Statistik von Baden 1996: 336–40).

6 For example, until 1973 a party needed 10 per cent of the vote in any of the seven regions (Regierungsbezirke) in order to qualify for representation. Since then the qualification has been 5 per cent in the whole Land of Bavaria. The Land parliament elected in 2003 was the first to be elected for a five-year term, and the number of seats was reduced from 205 (as it had been since 1950) to 180.

7 For example, in 1998 in the Oberbayern region Erwin Schneider was placed thirty-seventh on the CSU list, but his list vote total (he did not contest a constituency) was higher than nine candidates placed above him on the list. He was elected as fourth of ten successful list candidates. In the same region in 1998 Dr Hildegard Kronawitter, placed sixteenth on the SPD list, secured a remarkable 74,017 list votes (to add to her 12,212 constituency votes) and was elected as second candidate on the SPD list. Candidates placed fifth and seventh on that list were unsuccessful. Hildegard Hamm-Brücher (FDP) in 1962 moved from seventeenth place to first place because of use by voters of this option of voting for a particular candidate on a list (James 1988: 34). In

the 1978 election, it was estimated that 95 per cent of voters used the opportunity to vote for an individual on the list, rather than simply vote for the party list as a whole (Falter 1979: 52).

8 In Bavaria the dual vote system does not really benefit smaller parties, since there is no advantage in campaigning for split votes. The Greens, for example, would be helped to reach the qualifying 5 per cent of votes as much by constituency votes as by list votes, since parties require at least 5 per cent of Gesamtstimmen (the aggregate of the two kinds of votes) to obtain representation in the Land parliament.

9 A referendum on 13 June 2004 provided a clear majority in favour of a proposal to have a mixed-member electoral system, with seventy-one directly elected MdLs from seventeen constituencies, and the remaining fifty MdLs drawn from party lists to provide overall proportional representation. Especially unusual for Land elections are the provisions which (a) give each voter five votes in constituencies and five for Land lists, to use for one or more candidates in each case, allowing panachage as well as cumulative voting; and (b) to abandon the 5 per cent requirement for representation, so each party qualifying for even one seat under proportional representation will obtain that seat. Implementation of the proposal requires legislation in the Land legislature (*Das Parlament* 21 June 2004).

10 An exception is Mecklenburg-Vorpommern, where turnout has been unusually high in Land elections in 1998 (80.4 per cent) and 2002 (71.1 per cent), simply because the Land election took place on the same day as the Bundestag election.

11 By comparison, turnout in the 2003 elections to the Scottish Parliament was 49.4 per cent and to the Welsh Assembly 38.2 per cent.

12 This transfer process is facilitated by the lack of necessity for ministers to hold seats as elected members of the Bundestag. Without a seat, they can speak but not vote.

13 Though they point out that, due to some miscalculations by Dinkel, the two exceptional cases which they identify are not the two which Dinkel claimed to be exceptions in his article (Jeffery and Hough 2001: 81, 96).

7

Conclusion

The pervasiveness of electoral politics in Germany has been demonstrated in this book. Electoral politics in Germany affects not only the party composition of governing coalitions, but also the choice and timing of policies, the career plans of politicians, the prominence given by the media to election preparations and campaigns and to the published results of periodic opinion surveys and the activities and financial outlays of party headquarters. Since these election-related phenomena are apparent throughout the four-year cycle between Bundestag elections, it has been claimed that – as is the case in other countries – German politics is one continuous election campaign. Certainly there is evidence of this. A recent example is the manoeuvring of Angela Merkel, the chair of the CDU, immediately following the failure of the Christian Democrats to win the 2002 election, to position herself as the next chancellor-candidate for the CDU–CSU by claiming the leadership of the parliamentary party group in the Bundestag. This has resulted in pressure two years ahead of the next election for the Christian Democrats to make an early decision about who that chancellor-candidate should be. Policies are considered not only in terms of their merits or feasibility, but also in relation to their effect on voting behaviour in the next Bundestag election. The effect of the timing of elections on budgetary allocations in Germany has been analysed by a number of political scientists, and it has been demonstrated that spending decisions are affected by the proximity of the election date (Lessmann 1987). Because Germany is a federal state, parties and politicians not only have to adjust their behaviour to take account of the very predictable scheduling of Bundestag elections (every four years unless something very extraordinary occurs, as in 1972 and 1982). They have to adjust their behaviour to adapt to the numerous Land elections which are interspersed through that four-year period, elections whose outcomes may affect the ability of the government to pass legislation, because of the effect of those elections on party strength in the Bundesrat. Land elections are also seen as interim guides to the standing of the parties in the opinion of the electorate, and perhaps of the acceptability of particular coalitions or the popularity of particular politicians (especially those seen as possible chancellor-candidates).

So one controversial aspect of the notion of the 'permanent election campaign' in Germany is the large number of elections which take place, and the large number of 'election Sundays' which thus occur. In any five-year period there will be a Bundestag election, at least sixteen Land elections, an election to the EP and sixteen sets of local council elections: at least thirty-four in total, or one for every seven or eight weeks (assuming that each election were to be held on a different date). There have been proposals to reduce this 'permanent election campaigning'. Increasing the term of the Bundestag to five years would have little effect in itself, though would allow a government an additional year in which to bring forward less-popular policies before needing to plan its budget and policies with an eye to attracting votes.[1] Making all Land legislatures adopt a five-year term (which most of them now have) and bunching Land elections into two or three dates in the cycle would reduce the number of dates on which elections took place: at least to begin with. Nothing could prevent a Land legislature from being dissolved prematurely, as happened in Hesse (1983), Hamburg (1987, 1993, 2004) and Berlin (2001), for example, in which case the scheduled grouping of elections would start to unravel. In any case, some are opposed to such grouping, because it would reduce the serial effect of Land elections being periodic electoral tests of the popularity of the governing coalition and could mean that a temporary swing in the mood of the electorate at the time of a group of Land elections could have a vastly disproportional effect on, say, the balance of party strength in the Bundesrat.

Does any of this matter? Surely in representative democracies the continuous pressure on governments, parties and politicians to be sensitive to the wishes of the electorate and to the periodic expression of the wishes of the voters through elections can only be a good thing? That may be so. In a political system such as that in Germany, however, where corporatism is pervasive, where the notion of consensus is seen both as a politically preferable mode of policymaking and an often necessary means of passing legislation when the opposition parties in the Bundestag control a majority of votes in the Bundesrat, the necessity of trimming political decisions to the imperatives of electoral politics results in a reluctance to undertake radical reforms. Kitschelt has argued that in countries such as Germany (but also Austria, France and Italy, among others) where the party system is based on centripetal competition, reform of the welfare state and its entitlements poses a special challenge because of electoral politics. Either reform will be only incremental and marginal, or it will produce an electoral backlash which will result in the rejection of any government which attempts to be more radical (Kitschelt 2003: 134). In Germany, for example, this 'centripetal trap' is 'amplified by federal and bicameral fragmentation of the decision process' (Kitschelt 2003: 149).

One neglected function of elections which matters for the political parties is the excuse they offer for state financial aid to parties. Ever since the introduction of the Party Law in 1967, to fulfil after a long delay the instruction of Article 21 of the Basic Law to regulate by legislation the details of the constitutional provisions relating to political parties, parties have received state financial aid based in whole or in part on their relative performance in elections. Initially the subsidy for each party securing at least the qualifying level of 0.5 per cent of votes cast in Bundestag elections was linked to the number of votes received.[2] Later reforms amended the system, introducing a higher level of payment for the first tranche of votes (designed to help smaller parties and those not enjoying the benefits of the financial aid given to parties in the Bundestag), and adding a state 'bonus' to income received from subscriptions or donations. However, such subsidies were subject to a total overall limit, which was considerably less than the total sum to which the parties could lay claim under this system. This removed the incentive to maximise turnout, or to attract new members or donors. The total overall sum is subject to increases which allow for inflation in the cost of those activities which the parties undertake (e.g. staff salaries, travel costs, rents). Such increases are recommended by an independent commission of experts appointed by the president. The first such commission was appointed in 1995. These state subsidies are also paid to parties for Land and EP elections (the qualifying level for Land election subsidies is 1 per cent of the vote). However, proposals to extend the system to local council elections have been rejected by the parties in the Bundestag, since such payments would still be made within the limit of the overall total sum available and, because small parties and locally-confined parties would then benefit, the 'established' parties would lose out relatively (Herud 2001: 497).

The German electoral system: monument or model?

The German mixed-member electoral system has long been regarded as a suitable model for other political systems to adopt. It combines proportional distribution of seats to political parties with elected constituency representatives. New Zealand, Scotland, Wales and several of the countries of eastern Europe have adopted a version of the German electoral system. Does the German electoral system – still – function effectively in Germany? In terms of its constitutional functions, the answer must be in the affirmative. The electoral system provides citizens with the regular opportunity to elect representatives to the Bundestag. Indeed, it cleverly supplies representation for the citizen in terms of both a local constituency representative and a party of the voter's choice, provided that choice is of a party with sufficient support to win at least 5 per cent of votes nationally (or three constituency seats). The difficulty in dissolving the Bundestag prematurely restricts the ability of the government to manipulate policy and timing of the dissolution of the legislature in its own favour, unlike the power of the British prime minister in relation to the House of Commons. This protects the citizen, since it removes an advantage enjoyed by the governing parties. The electoral system provides legitimacy to the Bundestag, and therefore to the chancellor and the government installed by receiving the support of a majority in the Bundestag. The relatively low level of invalid voting seems to indicate that the electoral system is sufficiently simple to be easily comprehensible, though the high level of misunderstanding about the relative role of constituency and list votes casts doubt on that comprehensibility (see chapter 4).

In terms of political effectiveness, however, there is room for question. If a function of the electoral system is to allow the electorate the opportunity to deliver a verdict on the government's performance, and to either approve a further term of office for the incumbent coalition or replace the government by a different coalition, then the German electoral system has had questionable success. In fifteen Bundestag elections, the incumbent government at the time of the election has only once been totally replaced: in 1998, when the SPD and Greens displaced the Christian Democrat–FDP coalition. In one case (1969) the coalition was changed by the removal of one party (the CDU–CSU) and the addition of another (the FDP), accompanied by a transfer of the chancellorship from the CDU to the SPD, which could deserve the epithet *Machtwechsel* (change of power) which was applied to it at the time. Otherwise, elections have been followed by relatively minor adjustments to coalitions, if any change has taken place at all. In 1953 the party representing refugees and displaced persons (GB/BHE) was added to the coalition which had taken office in 1949. In 1961 the FDP became a partner in the governing coalition, whereas prior to the election the CDU–CSU had governed alone. Two instances of more significant changes in the government occurred between elections: in 1966 when the grand coalition replaced the Christian Democrat–FDP coalition and in 1982, when the CDU–CSU and FDP formed the government following a successful constructive vote of no confidence which removed Chancellor Schmidt from office. The unsuccessful constructive vote of no confidence in Chancellor Brandt in 1972 shows the lack of relationship between such mid-term changes of government and the views of the electorate. That vote took place in April 1972. In the premature Bundestag election held in November 1972, Brandt's SPD and its coalition partner, the FDP, enjoyed increased electoral support. The SPD for the first time became the largest single party in the Bundestag. So had the Christian Democrats succeeded in displacing Brandt, the outcome would have been contrary to the desires of the electorate.

The point of this survey of changes in governments is that Bundestag elections do not usually directly affect the composition of governments. The 1998 election was an exception, since relatively large transfers of support from the Christian Democrats and FDP to the SPD took place (the Greens lost vote-share in that election). In 1969 the new coalition partners (SPD and FDP) together had a slightly lower share of votes than they had had in 1965, though they had not then formed a coalition with each other. In 1976 both those parties lost vote-share and seats compared to 1972, yet remained in office, as happened to the Christian Democrats and FDP in 1994 compared to their result in 1990. So decline in voting support is usually insufficient to eject a coalition from power.

Three factors account for this evisceration of the electoral process as a means of changing governments. Two are to do with the political parties. Neither of the two large parties can normally attract sufficient votes to claim an absolute majority of Bundestag seats for itself alone, though the CDU–CSU managed this in 1957 and came close in terms of seats in 1953 (being two seats short of an overall majority). So coalitions are necessary. Second, the FDP, being pivotal in the party system, can sometimes decide, as in 1969, which of the two larger parties will provide the chancellor and form a coalition with the FDP.[3] In other cases, as in 1998 and 2002, the Greens are available to the SPD as junior partner in a coalition though, as they are not 'pivotal' in the party system, they cannot exercise the power of choice sometimes available to the FDP. Some qualifications have to be added to this analysis. The FDP, despite its pivotal position, dare not switch partners too frequently. In both cases where it has abandoned its former partner (1969 and 1982–83) it has been punished by the electorate, and many of its former supporters have then rejected the FDP before new supporters can be brought on board. Second, coalition choices are not made lightly. Usually the voters will know ahead of the election which pairings of parties will be available to them. Thus in 1998, for example, the incumbent coalition of the Christian Democrats and FDP was faced by a potential coalition between the SPD and Greens. This was in effect the choice also in 2002, though formally the FDP had declined to commit itself to a coalition partner ahead of the election. The third factor concerns the electoral system directly. Because it is a proportional representation system (though one with a restrictive 5 per cent condition) it lacks the exaggerative effect of the first-past-the-post system used in the United Kingdom for House of Commons elections and which results almost always in single-party majorities of seats being created by less than half the popular vote, or the two-ballot French system which also produces disproportional effects. This proportionality feature was the cause of the attempt by the grand coalition to switch to a majoritarian system in the 1960s (see chapter 2).

The electoral system possesses another function related to electoral politics: to allow the voter a means of expression. 'All power emanates from the people', according to the Basic Law, and this power shall be exercised (*inter alia*) by elections and voting (Article 20 (1), (2)). In the eyes of some critics, the dominance of the parties in the political system constitutes one barrier to elections being a medium of expression for citizens. Those parties control the system of candidate selection; they control the legislative process (especially concerning laws affecting the remuneration and other benefits given to elected legislators, and the regulation of party financing and state subsidies), and they influence all three supposedly separate branches of government (the legislative, executive and judicial branches). They have thus, it is claimed, created a 'system' which renders useless the methods by which citizens might be expected to express their political views effectively (von Arnim 2001). The theoretically free formation of political parties is restricted by the strict legal requirements of the Party Law and, even when parties are formed and acquire official recognition under the Party Law, they find it difficult to succeed electorally because of the 5 per cent clauses in the federal and Länder electoral laws. The choices facing voters at elections thus tend to be among four or five parties at most, in terms of those with a realistic chance of winning seats, and several of these parties agree fairly closely on key issues within a political system which places a high value on consensus. Voters must choose between a pair of coalitions, one of which will form the government and be likely to remain in power for a decade or more. One indication that such criticisms are not just theoretical objections by those wishing for more direct democracy and a rather different electoral system is the decline in electoral participation since the 1980s and the lack of trust in, and respect for, politicians on the part of the electorate.

Elections as 'bread and circuses'?

Does it matter if, in the German system, elections rarely change governments and that they are not effective means of expressing public opinion? After all, the German political system enjoys a multiplicity of press and broadcasting media through which opinions can be expressed. Perhaps not. Despite the economic and social problems besetting the FRG since reunification, there are few signs that support for the political system is at dangerously low levels. One survey of western German respondents found that in 1989 88 per cent were satisfied with the democratic system; in 1993 this had declined, but only to 78 per cent (Zelle 1995: 334). Electoral turnout is still reasonably high, compared to other western democracies where there is not compulsory voting. There is no apparent pressure for a different kind of political system. Electoral support for the PDS in eastern Germany or for extreme right-wing parties is seen as primarily an expression of protest against the 'establishment' parties, rather than as a Weimar-like flight to ideological politics. Participation in political movements and interest-group politics is still at 'normal' levels, even though party membership is declining. With this diagnosis, Bundestag elections can be seen as events which interest the public, in which they can still express their partisan choices, and where – even though a change of government may well not result from the election – changes in the balance of strength among parties can be registered, which may have future consequences. For example, it became clear to the FDP in the early 1980s that declining support for the SPD might well drag the FDP down as well, so a change of coalition was advisable, and the Greens learned from their 1990 exclusion from the Bundestag that the only chance they had was to reduce or eliminate the influence of the 'fundamentalist' wing in the party. And even though Bundestag elections rarely change governments, Land elections do, quite often, which may be a satisfactory substitute for the electorate.

On the other hand, it can be argued that elections should, from time to time, result in changes of government. This might mean that Germany would need to change its electoral system (a reform for which there seems to be little support). It also means that Bundestag elections especially may be seen by cynics as 'bread and circuses': an expensive diversion for the electorate, but which mean little in terms of the distribution of political power which is firmly in the hands of elites, or the determining of important political decisions. Whether concerning entry into the EU single-currency system, deployment of German military forces in the former Yugoslavia, reforms to the system of unemployment insurance or new and restrictive environmental legislation, the opinions of the electorate are ignored. They can be ignored safely because an incumbent government is likely to be confirmed in office by a Bundestag election. It is true that the Bundesrat, on some issues especially, may obstruct legislation or modify it, and that makes Land elections more important at times than they would otherwise be (in terms of creating opposition majorities, for instance). However, there seems to be no satisfactory solution to the problem of the unimportance of Bundestag elections and the insignificance of the opinions of the electorate, unless that solution is the introduction of more 'direct democracy'.

Some of the criticism of the ability of the electoral system to represent the wishes of the people might be abated were there to be more opportunities for direct democracy in Germany. The issue of adoption of the EU constitution, to be ratified by referendum in many countries, including the United Kingdom, provoked a discussion in 2004 concerning the need to amend the Basic Law in order to permit the use of referendums on this and other issues in the FRG. At present, the Basic Law makes no allowance for national referendums (except on matters of revision of Länder territory). However, most of the Länder have constitutional provision for referendums, on matters concerning the Land as a whole, and, in many cases, in local authority areas (Weixner 2002: 101–12). There have been several examples in the FRG of referendums on issues concerning the territorial boundaries of Länder: that concerning the creation of Baden-Württemberg in 1950 (and Baden in 1970), in areas of Rhineland-Pfalz in 1956, in parts of each of the five 'new' Länder in 1990, following the decision to link the former GDR with the FRG, and the issue of the merger of Berlin and Brandenburg in 1996. In addition, Brandenburg in 1992 and Thuringia and Mecklenburg-Vorpommern in 1994 held plebiscites on adoption of their post-reunification Länder constitutions (Weixner 2002: 127 35). So direct democracy is not utterly foreign to the German political system, and a limited provision of referendums at the level of national politics might well be a gain for German democracy.

Does 'electoral politics' matter?

Obviously the answer must be that it does matter. It can matter in terms of changing governments (though that has been rare in Bundestag elections). It matters in terms of providing citizens with an opportunity to participate in selecting representatives (though incumbency rates are quite high, so there is not much of a turnover of MdBs). It matters in focusing attention on political choices at least once every four years. It matters in bestowing legitimacy on the political institutions and processes of the political system. The attention given to electoral politics over the four years of an electoral cycle by the parties, by politicians, by opinion research institutes, by the mass media and sometimes by the Constitutional Court indicates the importance of electoral politics.

There are more subtle ways in which electoral politics can be important. Even if actual decision-making power is concentrated in the hands of the chancellor (the 'chancellor government' thesis), or the cabinet, the coalition committee or the party hierarchy, together with civil servants and advisors closest to the government, the discipline and restraints imposed by electoral politics serve as an important constraining factor in their exercise of power. Accepting the extent to which politics in Germany is 'elite politics', accepting the frequency with which financial improprieties have been revealed which tarnish politicians or their parties, accepting the degree of self-serving legislation which politicians introduce concerning their remuneration, pension rights and other advantages, the fact that they can only influence, but not control, the opinions of the voters on election day is a vital ingredient in German politics, the basis upon which its claim to be a democracy rests.

Notes

1   For example, an Expert Commission on Constitutional Reform in 1976 rejected the idea of a five-year term (*Weser Kurier* 30 July 1976). The SPD

revived the idea in 1998, but without securing support for it (*Suddeutsche Zeitung* 6 November 1998).

2   Other Bundestag elections when the FDP could, arithmetically, have formed a governing coalition with either the CDU–CSU or the SPD were in 1965, 1972, 1976 and 1980. However, the FDP in advance of the election had made a clear coalition commitment to remain with its existing partner (with which it was already in government) at each of these elections.

3   The sum was calculated according to the size of the whole electorate, whether voting or not. So at, say, DM5 per elector, a party receiving 1 million votes but where turnout was only 50 per cent would receive DM10 million (i.e. DM10 for each vote it actually received).

Appendix 1
Turnout and the allocation of seats to Länder

The Electoral Law prescribes the total number of seats in the Bundestag. Since 2002 this has been 596, plus any additional surplus seats (of which there were five in the Bundestag election in 2002). Since these 596 seats are divided on a 50:50 basis between constituency seats and seats allocated from party lists, it might be assumed that each Land should also have an equal number of constituency seats and list seats (apart from any surplus seats at a particular election). However, two factors can render this assumption false.

First, constituency seats are allocated to each Land based on its total population of German citizens. In the redistribution of seats which was necessarily combined with the reduction in the size of the Bundestag from 656 following reunification to 596, every Land lost some constituency seats, but the 'new' Länder of the former GDR had to lose proportionally more seats because of greater declines in population. For example, Bremen, Hamburg, Saarland and Schleswig-Holstein lost only one seat each, whereas every 'new' Land lost two seats each, except Saxony, which lost three. (Berlin, a mixture of the former GDR and the 'old' FRG, lost just one seat). Saxony-Anhalt, Brandenburg and Thuringia have approximately the same population each as Schleswig-Holstein (and each of these Länder has ten constituency seats), while Mecklenburg-Vorpommern (now seven constituencies) has a similar population size to Hamburg (which has six constituencies). However, the allocation of list seats to each Land depends on turnout of voters in the election. So if a Land has a relatively high proportion of inhabitants below voting age, it will secure fewer list seats than constituency seats even if its turnout rate is average. This is because a turnout rate of 75 per cent of the electorate may mean only 50 per cent of the inhabitants voting in the case of that Land, compared to the same turnout representing 60 per cent of the inhabitants in some other

Land of equal population size but possessed of fewer citizens below voting age.

Second, turnout rates vary substantially among the Länder, and especially between the 'new' Länder in what was formerly the GDR, which have tended to have relatively low turnout rates, and the 'old' Länder of western Germany. In 2002, as in every Bundestag election since reunification, turnout rates in all the Länder of eastern Germany were below those of the western German Länder. In western Germany, turnout in 2002 was 80.7 per cent; in eastern Germany it was 72.8 per cent. The average for the whole FRG was 79.1 per cent. The lowest turnout in a Land in western Germany was in Bremen (78.9 per cent) and the highest in eastern Germany was Thuringia (74.8 per cent).

This meant that in the 2002 election every Land in eastern Germany (including Berlin) had fewer list seats than constituency seats, and every Land in western Germany more list seats than constituency seats, apart from Schleswig-Holstein, Bremen and Rhineland-Pfalz, which had equal numbers of list and constituency seats. The ratio in Mecklenburg-Vorpommern was only 42.9 per cent of the list seats which it should have had on an equality basis (three list seats, seven constituencies), and Brandenburg had only 60 per cent of its 'normal' allowance (six list seats, ten constituency seats). Lower Saxony, on the other hand, had 17 per cent more list seats (thirty-four, compared to twenty-nine constituencies) and Bavaria 15.9 per cent more (fifty-one list seats, but only forty-four constituency seats), mainly because of high relative turnout.

The uneven ratios of list seats compared to constituency seats in eastern Germany is one reason why since 1990 such a high proportion of surplus seats has been found in the 'new' Länder. It becomes easier for one party to win all the constituency seats on fewer than 50 per cent of the vote, and there are insufficient list seats to provide proportional representation for other parties. In 1990 all six surplus seats, in 1994 thirteen of the sixteen, in 1998 nine out of thirteen and in 2002 four out of five were in Länder in eastern Germany (see Appendix 2).

Appendix 2
The causes of surplus seats at Bundestag elections

The phenomenon of surplus seats (Überhangmandate) received little attention prior to the reunification of Germany. At no election before 1990 were there more than five such seats (in 1961). In the elections between 1965 and 1976 there were no such seats. In no election did surplus seats come close to playing a role in deciding which party or coalition of parties would possess a majority in the Bundestag.

In 1990, things changed. At that election there were six surplus seats. In 1994 there were sixteen and in 1998 thirteen such seats. In 2002 the number of surplus seats fell to five. In 1994 surplus seats almost decided whether the Kohl government (a coalition of the Christian Democrats and the liberal FDP) could continue to govern, since twelve surplus seats went to the CDU and only four to the SPD, a net gain of eight seats for the CDU. These extra eight seats gave the governing coalition 341 seats, the other parties (SPD, Greens and PDS) 331: a majority of ten seats which, without surplus seats, would otherwise have been a majority of just two seats. In 2002 the net gain of three surplus seats (four for the SPD, one for the CDU) enlarged the majority of the SPD–Green coalition from six seats to nine seats. So in both 1994 and 2002 small shifts in voting behaviour, or the addition or subtraction of a small number of surplus seats, could have prevented the incumbent coalition government from continuing in office.

Surplus seats distort the proportionality of the German electoral system since, unlike electoral systems in the Länder (see chapter 6), there is no provision for 'equalisation' seats to be allocated to other parties. If a party in a Land election in, for example, Thuringia or Baden-Württemberg, is allocated surplus seats, then further additional seats are awarded to other parties until proportionality of the overall allocation of seats is restored. In Bundestag elections, that does not occur. Apart from the 5 per cent requirement for qualification for allotments of list seats, this is the only significant distortion of what otherwise is a system of accurate proportional representation of parties. In 2002 the SPD (the principal beneficiary of surplus seats) was awarded one seat for every 73,644 votes. The CSU needed 74,336 votes and the CDU 74,548 for each seat. The Greens needed 74,697 and the FDP 75,265 votes for each seat.

The causes of surplus seats are varied. One cause is the different basis for calculating how many constituency seats each Land possesses (according to its population), contrasted with the number of its list seats (based on voting turnout). So, even ignoring differences in turnout, discrepancies in these two factors of total population and population of voting age can result in some Länder having more, and others fewer, constituency seats compared to list seats (see Appendix 1). When differential turnout is added into the equation, that discrepancy can increase considerably. In 2002, Saxony-Anhalt had ten constituency seats, but only eight list seats. The SPD in that Land won all ten constituencies (56 per cent of seats) but obtained only 43 per cent of list votes: so was entitled to no more than eight seats. The two additional seats became surplus seats in the calculation of total seats won by the SPD.

Vote-splitting is another factor. Since list seats (and the total number of seats for a party) are awarded on the basis of second votes, but constituency seats are won by first votes, discrepancies in a party's share of first and second votes can give it more constituency victories than its share of second votes would justify. The biggest parties (CDU and SPD) tend to have more first votes than second votes, since 'vote-splitters' (see chapter 5) are either supporters of those larger parties who 'lend' their second vote to the smaller coalition partner party (usually now the FDP for the CDU, the Greens for the SPD), or supporters of those smaller parties voting 'rationally' with their first vote for a constituency candidate of the larger coalition partner likely to win the seat. So even if a party wins all ten constituency seats in a Land with 50 per cent of first votes, and assuming a total of twenty seats in that Land, then if it only has 45 per cent of list votes (an entitlement of nine seats in total), one of its constituency victories would constitute a surplus seat. Indeed, a party can win all the constituency seats (generally 45–55 per cent of seats available in a Land) on a relatively small share of the list votes in that Land. In Saxony in 2002 there were seventeen constituency seats and twelve list seats, making a total of twenty-nine seats. Though winning only 33.6 per cent of list votes, the CDU in Saxony in 2002 won thirteen of the seventeen constituencies in that Land. Thirteen as a percentage of twenty-nine is 45 per cent. So one of the constituency seats was a surplus seat for the CDU.

Saxony was also affected by a third causal factor: the strength of 'third parties'. So in several constituencies the PDS obtained between 18 and 20 per cent of constituency votes, without winning a seat. The SPD in seats won by the CDU sometimes obtained between 30 per cent and 34 per cent. So CDU constituency seats were often won with only between 33 and 40 per cent of first votes.

Finally, in Länder with very small numbers of seats, such as Bremen (2002: four seats in total), a surplus seat can arise because the method of calculating seats results in large arithmetic remainders, and one of these can give rise to a surplus seat, as happened in Bremen in 1994. Indeed, it has been calculated that, in certain circumstances, a paradox can arise. If a party which, having won most of the constituency seats in a Land, had polled fewer list votes in that Land than it actually did, it could end up with extra seats in total (assuming the same national total of votes in each case). This is because it would retain all the constituency seats, more of which would become surplus seats, but win additional seats in other Länder because of the method of allocating a party's seats among the Land lists.

There is an almost metaphysical dispute as to which kind of seats are surplus seats. Some claim that they are constituency seats (after all, the party wins more such seats than its total allocation in that Land, so it would seem that the constituency seats are 'surplus'). Others point out that the number of constituency seats remains constant with or without surplus seats, so that the extra seats are additional list seats. Therefore surplus seats must be list seats won inequitably by the benefiting party (though which list seats these are is difficult to establish for, by definition, they are not in the Land where the surplus seats seem to have been won). The Constitutional Court seemed to favour, implicitly, the first interpretation. In 1998 it ruled unanimously that in a Land where a party has won surplus seats, should a vacancy occur – by, for example, the death of an MdB from that party – no successor can fill the vacancy until the number of seats for that party in that Land returns to normal. This applies whether the vacancy is in a constituency seat or on the party Land list. So in 1998 the Bundestag began with 669 MdBs (the standard 656 plus thirteen surplus seat MdBs). In 2002 it had been reduced to 665, because four vacancies had remained unfilled following the 1998 Constitutional Court ruling.

Appendix 3

The 'three-seat' alternative to the 5 per cent requirement

There is a 'three-seat' alternative to the requirement that parties must obtain 5 per cent of list votes to qualify for an allocation of list seats. This dates back to the 1949 Bundestag election, where winning one constituency was sufficient to by-pass the 5 per cent requirement (which then operated in each Land separately). The justification for this alternative qualification was that a party which showed local or regional strength, sufficient to win a constituency, should be given proportional representation in the Bundestag. In 1956 the law changed, so that parties from then on required three seats within the FRG to by-pass the 5 per cent requirement. However, critics point to the fact that a party need not win three seats in the same region: they could be in Hamburg, Saxony and Saarland, so the justification on the grounds of regional strength is demonstrably invalid. Critics claim that there is no justification for a party with 4 per cent of list votes (but three constituency victories) being awarded list seats, yet a party with 4.9 per cent of list votes (but maybe no constituency seats) being denied list seats.

The only parties to benefit from the three-seat alternative were the DP in 1956 – though only thanks to an electoral pact with the CDU which gave the DP 'safe' constituency seats without CDU competition – and the PDS in 1994. In 1998 the PDS won sufficient second votes to qualify without needing this alternative qualification. In 2002 it only won two seats, but as it received below 5 per cent of list votes had no additional seats awarded to it. Under the one-seat rule in 1949 and 1953 some small parties benefited, but again sometimes electoral pacts with the CDU played a role.

Appendix 4
The official representative electoral statistics

Psephologists concerned with elections to the Bundestag have had the benefit of a special form of data not found in many other democracies: the official representative electoral statistics. These have been collected since 1953, with the exceptions of the elections of 1994 and 1998, when concerns about data protection gave rise to legislation prohibiting the collection of such statistical information. These data are collected by the Federal Statistical Office, based on representative samples of polling stations. In selected polling districts, ballot papers are coded with information concerning (a) the gender and (b) the age-group of the voter. On this basis, data can be collated concerning turnout for each age-group classified by gender, and regarding the party vote and any split-voting for the same categories. Post-election validation exercises have found that the samples chosen give outcomes very close to the actual result, after allowance is made for postal voting (Jesse 1987: 232–3). Though gender and age-group are only two of the many possible significant distinctive demographic and social characteristics which are required for analyses of voting behaviour, they do provide useful data, and act as a reliable source for cross-checking of survey data, for example.

Appendix 5
The election of the federal president

The Basic Law provides for the method of election of the federal president. The president is elected by an electoral college (the *Bundesversammlung*) composed of (a) all the members of the Bundestag, plus (b) a number of representatives from each Land equivalent to the number of seats in the Bundestag allocated to each Land. Though these Land representatives are normally drawn from Land parliaments, they can be prominent personalities without a parliamentary seat. Representatives are allotted to the parties according to the proportional strength of each party in the Land parliament. For the election in 2004 there were 1,205 members of the electoral college (one MdB died and it was too late for a replacement to be nominated). There can be as many as three rounds of balloting. An absolute majority of votes (in 2004: 603) is required for election on the first two rounds; a simple majority is sufficient for election if a third round is required. Once elected, a president can serve only two terms consecutively. In 2004 the CDU–CSU had 539 votes; the SPD had 459; the Greens 90; the FDP 83; the PDS 31; and there were three others. Horst Köhler, the candidate supported by the Christian Democrats and FDP, defeated Gesine Schwan, supported by the left-wing parties, by 604 to 589 on the first round of balloting. Presidential elections may be of importance directly: the president has certain reserve powers as well as ceremonial and formal powers broadly equivalent to a constitutional monarch, and possesses influence that can be exercised publicly or 'behind the scenes'. Examples of such influence include Heuss' veto of Dehler's reappointment as Justice Minister in 1953; Lübke's openly expressed preference for a 'grand coalition' in the 1960s; and von Weizsäcker's critique of political parties in 1992. They can be of indirect importance. The support of the CDU and CSU for Heuss (leader of the FDP) as candidate for the presidency in 1949 was a bargaining chip in coalition negotiations which led to the formation of the first coalition government. The FDP's decision to support Heinemann (SPD) rather than Schröder (CDU) in 1969 was a clear signal that the FDP was available for the first time as a coalition partner for the SPD following the Bundestag election later that year, should the outcome of the election have permitted such a coalition.

Appendix 6
d'Hondt or Hare–Niemeyer?
That is the question

For Bundestag and Land parliament elections, there is a requirement that seats be allocated proportionately among qualifying parties (i.e. parties which have secured at least 5 per cent of list votes or, in Bundestag elections, won three constituencies). However, vote shares will always mean that parties will have entitlements to fractional parts of seats. How can a fair method be devised to decide which parties obtain the last two seats when they have, say, vote shares of 44.2, 42.6, 7.7 and 5.5 per cent? In a parliament of 100 seats the first party will win 44 seats, the second party 42, the third party 7 and the fourth party 5. This leaves two seats still to be allocated.

The d'Hondt method, used in Bundestag elections until a change in the Electoral Law in 1985, lists the total votes for parties in order, then divides the total vote by successive integers (1, 2, 3 . . .). For this result the outcome would be:

Party	A	B	C	D
Vote	44.2	42.6	7.7	5.5
Divided by 2	22.1	21.3	3.55	2.55
Divided by 3	14.7	14.2	2.57	1.83, etc.

Taking the highest quotients, Party A wins the first seat, Party B the second, Party A the third (22.1), Party B the fourth (21.3), etc.

Which party wins the 99th and 100th seats? The vote-share of Party A divided by 45 (i.e. one more than the 44 seats already allocated) gives a quotient of 0.9822. That of Party B divided by 43 gives a quotient of 0.9906. Party C has a quotient of 0.9625 (i.e. 7.7 divided by 8) and Party D a quotient of 0.9167 (5.5 divided by 6). So Party B wins the 99th seat, Party A the 100th seat.

Using Hare–Niemeyer, the outcome is different. This method uses an equation:

$$\text{Party seats} = \frac{\text{Total number of seats} \times \text{votes for the party}}{\text{Total number of votes}}$$

So, using the same percentages given in the d'Hondt example, the outcomes would be as before: Party A 44 seats, Party B 42, Party C 7 and Party D 5, but the remaining two seats would be awarded to the parties with the highest fractional remainders: so Party C (0.7 remaining after seven seats awarded) and Party B (0.6 remaining) would obtain the 99th and 100th seats. Comparing the results:

	A	B	C	D
d'Hondt	45	43	7	5
Hare-Niemeyer	44	43	8	5

Appendix 7
The Bundesrat powers of veto

The Bundesrat is composed of representatives of the governments of the Länder. Each Land has between three and six votes in the Bundesrat, depending on population size. North Rhine-Westphalia and Bavaria have six votes each, Hesse five and Bremen three, for example. These votes must be bestowed as a package: a Land with five votes cannot, for instance, give four votes in favour and one vote against a proposal because coalition partners cannot agree. All five votes must be given one way or another, or withheld entirely. The Bundesrat must give its consent to all legislation.

However, legislation is divided into two types. Legislation where the consent of the Bundesrat is not necessary (*nichtzustimmungsbedürftige Gesetze*) can be rejected by the Bundesrat, but if the Bundestag votes to override the Bundesrat by an absolute majority it can do so. Should the Bundesrat vote against legislation in this category by a two-thirds majority, a similar two-thirds majority in the Bundestag is needed to override such a veto. Legislation which in any way affects the powers and responsibilities of the Länder requires the consent of the Bundesrat and its veto cannot be overridden by the Bundestag (*zustimmungsbedürftige Gesetze*). Where such a veto is exercised, the differences between the two chambers may be resolved by means of the Mediation Committee (*Vermittlungsauschuss*) composed of sixteen representatives of each chamber.

A two-thirds majority of the Bundesrat is also needed (with a similar majority in the Bundestag) to pass amendments to the Basic Law.

Appendix 8

The Bundestag Election: 2005

The premature Bundestag election on 18 September 2005 was unusual for seven reasons. First, the decision in May 2005 by Chancellor Schröder to seek a premature dissolution of the Bundestag was a surprise. Second, the validity of that decision required a verdict from the Constitutional Court. Third, for the first time a female politician – Angela Merkel – was chancellor-candidate. Fourth, for the first time since 1983 a new party was likely to win seats in the Bundestag: the Left party, an alliance between the PDS, led by Gysi, and – mainly western German – left-wing socialists led by the former SPD leader, Lafontaine. Fifth, the result, especially for the Christian Democrats, confounded all expectations, including those of the leading opinion survey research firms. Sixth, the final result was not known for a fortnight, since it depended on a postponed election in a Dresden constituency. Seventh, a 'grand coalition' was the outcome, for the first time following an election, and only the second time in the history of the FRG.

Schröder decided to seek a dissolution of the Bundestag following the election in North Rhine-Westphalia on 22 May 2005, which continued the trend of disastrous Land election results for the SPD–Green party coalition. Discontent in his own party concerning labour market reforms, which his government sought to introduce, tempted Schröder to seek a new mandate. This decision was not fully supported either within the SPD or by many within the Green party. A schedule was conceived, which was designed to lead to a Bundestag election on 18 September 2005 by means of an artificial defeat in a vote of confidence in the government in July, followed by a request to the president to dissolve the Bundestag. However, two MdBs laid a complaint before the Constitutional Court. This concerned the constitutionality of the decision by the federal president to dissolve the Bundestag, since Schröder's government still enjoyed a safe majority and indeed that majority passed legislation even after the loss of the vote of confidence. In August, the Constitutional Court upheld the decision of the president, in effect stating that the president could not look beyond the fact of the defeat of the vote of confidence (*Die Welt*, 26 August 2005). This verdict seemed to grant the chancellor a power of dissolution which the Bundestag itself did not enjoy.

The decision by the Christian Democrats to confirm Merkel as chancellor-candidate meant that a female and Protestant chancellor-candidate, and one originally from the GDR, would lead their campaign. Apparently none of these personal characteristics made much difference to voting behaviour, though Merkel's decisions during the campaign, especially concerning radical economic reforms such as a move towards a simplified tax system, her unconvincing performance in the televised debate against the chancellor and her lacklustre campaign style, probably did cost votes. Though the Christian Democrats until the last days of the campaign enjoyed a comfortable lead in opinion surveys and seemed likely (though not certain) to be able to form a coalition with the FDP, the result surprised most people. As anticipated, the SPD and Greens suffered losses; the Left party composed of the PDS and left-wing socialists obtained a substantial share of the vote; the FDP had an unexpectedly good result. However, the Christian Democrats suffered a catastrophic decline in vote-share and obtained their second-lowest share of the vote since 1949. Their lead over the SPD was just one per cent and four Bundestag seats. Consequently, the only realistic coalition combinations which could command a majority were either a 'grand coalition' of the CDU–CSU and SPD, or a novel coalition of the CDU–CSU, FDP and Greens (called a 'Jamaica coalition' because the black, yellow and green colours of that nation's flag corresponded to the colours of the parties of the prospective coalition). The SPD had reiterated that they would not form a coalition containing the Left party. The 'Jamaica' option failed to win enthusiasm from the Greens, so, after three weeks of bargaining during which the SPD tried to insist on Schröder's right to remain as chancellor, it was agreed to form a 'grand coalition' under the leadership of Merkel. The SPD obtained the same number of cabinet posts as the CDU–CSU, including the important ministries responsible for justice, finance and employment.

The Dresden election (postponed due to the death of a nominated candidate) produced some remarkable tactical voting. Many voters who supported the victorious CDU constituency candidate voted for the FDP list. In this way they protected the surplus seats allocated to the CDU in

Saxony. Had the CDU list won extra votes, one of its surplus seats would have been lost. The SPD won nine surplus seats, the CDU seven. Eleven of those seats were in eastern Germany.

Following the election in the Dresden constituency the final result was: Christian Democrats 35.2 per cent (226 seats); SPD 34.2 per cent (222 seats); FDP 9.8 per cent (61 seats); Left party 8.7 per cent (54 seats); Greens 8.1 per cent (51 seats). Turnout was 77.7 per cent.

Bibliography

Published in German

Abromeit, H. and K. Burkhardt, 'Die Wählerinitiativen im Wahlkampf 1972', in D. Just and L. Romain, eds, *Auf der Suche nach dem mündigen Wähler* (Bonn: Bundeszentrale für politische Bildung, 1974).

Arzheimer, K. and J. Falter, 'Ist der Osten wirklich rot? Das Wahlverhalten bei der Bundestagswahl 2002 in Ost-West-Perspektive', *Aus Politik und Zeitgeschichte, Beilage: Das Parlament*, no. 49/50 (2002).

Baring, A., *Machtwechsel* (Stuttgart: Deutsche Verlags-Anstalt, 1982).

Behnke, J., 'Von Überhangmandaten und Gesetzlücken', *Aus Politik und Zeitgeschichte, Beilage: Das Parlament*, no. 52 (2003).

Beyer, H.-J., 'Der Bundestagswahlkampf 1976 der FDP', *Zeitschrift für Parlamentsfragen*, 10 (1979).

Bieber, C., *Politische Projekte im Internet* (Frankfurt/Main: Campus, 1999).

Boll, B. and A. Römmele, 'Strukturelle Vorteile der Amtsinhaber? Wahlchancen von Parlamentariern im international Vergleich', *Zeitschrift für Parlamentsfragen*, 25 (1994).

Bösch, F., 'Bereit für den Wechsel? Die strategische und inhaltliche Positionierung von CDU/CSU und FDP vor der Bundestagswahl 2002', *Aus Politik und Zeitgeschichte, Beilage: Das Parlament*, no. 21 (2002).

Bundeswahlleiter, Der, *Sonderheft: Die Wahlbewerber für die Wahl zum 13. Deutschen Bundestag am 16. Oktober 1994* (Stuttgart: Metzler Poschel, 1994).

Bundeswahlleiter, Der, *Wahl zum 13. Deutschen Bundestag am 16. Oktober 1994. Heft 5: Textliche Auswertung der Wahlergebnisse* (Stuttgart: Metzler Poschel, 1995).

Bundeswahlleiter, Der, *Wahl zum 15. Deutschen Bundestag am 22. September 2002. Heft 5: Textliche Auswertung der Wahlergebnisse* (Stuttgart: Metzler Poschel, 2003).

Bürklin, W. and D. Roth, eds, *Das Superwahljahr* (Cologne: Bund-Verlag, 1994).

Busch, J. and F. Lüke, *Wir hatten die Wahl: Die Parteien im Kampf um die Macht 1965* (Munich: Günter Olzog Verlag, 1965).

Dinkel, R., 'Der Zusammenhang zwischen Bundes- und Landtagswahlergebnissen', *Politische Vierteljahresschrift*, 18 (1977).

Eilfort, M., *Die Nichtwähler – Wahlenthaltung als Form des Wahlverhaltens* (Paderborn: Schöningh, 1994).

Elff, M., 'Neue Mitte oder alte Lager? Welche Rolle spielen sozioökonomische Konfliktlinien für der Wahlergebnis von 1998?', in J. van Deth., H. Rattinger and E. Roller, eds, *Die Republik auf dem Weg zur Normalität* (Opladen: Leske & Budrich, 2000).

Erbe, F., 'Vierzehn Jahre Wahlen in Westdeutschland', in Sternberger, D., ed., *Wahlen und Wähler in Westdeutschland* (Villingen: Ring-Verlag, 1960).

Falter, J., 'Die bayerische Landtagswahl vom 15. Oktober 1978: anti-Strauss-Wahl oder Mobilisierungsschwäche einer "Staatspartei"?', *Zeitschrift für Parlamentsfragen*, 10 (1979).

Falter, J., 'Kontinuität und Neubeginn: Die Bundestagswahl 1949 zwischen Weimar und Bonn', *Politische Vierteljahresschrift*, 22 (1981).

Feist, U., 'Die Partei der Nichtwähler', *Gegenwartskunde*, 41 (1992).

Feist, U., 'Nichtwähler 1994: Eine Analyse der Bundestagswahl 1994', *Aus Politik und Zeitgeschichte, Beilage: Das Parlament*, no. 51–52 (1994).

Feist, U. and Liepelt, K. 'Stärkung und Gefährdung der sozialliberalen Koalition: Das Ergebnis der Bundestagswahl vom 5. Oktober 1980', *Zeitschrift für Parlamentsfragen*, 12 (1981).

Feldkamp, M., 'Deutscher Bundestag 1983 bis 2002/03: Parlaments- und Wahlstatistik', *Zeitschrift für Parlamentsfragen*, 34 (2003).

Forschungsgruppe Wahlen, *Bundestagswahl: Eine Analyse der Wahl vom 3. Oktober 1976* (Mannheim: Forschungsgruppe Wahlen, 1976).

Forschungsgruppe Wahlen, *Bundestagswahl: Eine Analyse der Wahl vom 5. Oktober 1980* (Mannheim: Forschungsgruppe Wahlen, 1980).

Forschungsgruppe Wahlen, *Bundestagswahl: Eine Analyse der Wahl vom 6. März 1983* (Mannheim: Forschungsgruppe Wahlen, 1983).

Forschungsgruppe Wahlen, *Bundestagswahl: Eine Analyse der Wahl vom 25. Januar 1987* (Mannheim: Forschungsgruppe Wahlen, 1987).

Forschungsgruppe Wahlen, *Bundestagswahl 1990: Eine Analyse der ersten gesamtdeutschen Bundestagswahl am 2. Dezember 1990* (Mannheim: Forschungsgruppe Wahlen, 1990).

Forschungsgruppe Wahlen, *Bundestagswahl: Eine Analyse der Wahl vom 16 Oktober 1994* (Mannheim: Forschungsgruppe Wahlen, 1994).

Forschungsgruppe Wahlen, *Bundestagswahl: Eine Analyse der Wahl vom 27. September 1998* (Mannheim: Forschungsgruppe Wahlen, 1998).

Forschungsgruppe Wahlen, *Europawahl am 13. Juni 1999* (Mannheim: Forschungsgruppe Wahlen, 1999).

Forschungsgruppe Wahlen, *Wahl in Baden-Württemberg* (Mannheim: Forschungsgruppe Wahlen, 2001).

Forschungsgruppe Wahlen, *Bundestagswahl: Eine Analyse der Wahl vom 22. September 2002* (Mannheim: Forschungsgruppe Wahlen, 2002).

Forschungsgruppe Wahlen, *Wahl in Bayern* (Mannheim: Forschungsgruppe Wahlen, 2003).

Forschungsgruppe Wahlen, *Europawahl am 13. Juni 2004* (Mannheim: Forschungsgruppe Wahlen, 2004a).

Forschungsgruppe Wahlen, *Wahl in Hamburg* (Mannheim: Forschungsgruppe Wahlen, 2004b).

Forschungsgruppe Wahlen, *Wahl in Brandenburg* (Mannheim: Forschungsgruppe Wahlen, 2004c).

Forschungsgruppe Wahlen, *Wahl in Sachsen* (Mannheim: Forschungsgruppe Wahlen, 2004d).

Gabriel, O. and F. Brettschneider, 'Soziale Konflikte und Wahlverhalten: Die erste gesamtdeutsche Bundestagswahl im Kontext der längerfristigen Entwicklung des Parteiensystems der Bundesrepublik Deustchland', in H. Rattinger, O. Gabriel and W. Jagodzinski, eds, *Wahlen und politische Einstellungen im vereinigten Deutschland* (Frankfurt/Main: Peter Lang, 1994).

Grotz, F. 'Die personalisierte Verhältniswahl unter den Bedingungen des gesamtdeutschen Parteiensystems: Eine Analyse der Entstehungsursachen von Überhangmandaten seit der Wiedervereinigung', *Politische Vierteljahresschrift*, 41 (2000).

Handschell, C., *Abgeordnete in Bund und Länder: Mitgliedschaft und Sozialstruktur 1946–1990* (Düsseldorf: Droste, 2002).

Hartenstein, W., 'Fünf Jahrzehnten Wahlen in der Bundesrepublik: Stabilität und Wandel', *Aus Politik und Zeitgeschichte, Beilage: Das Parlament*, no. 21 (2002).

Hebecker, E., 'Experimentieren für den Ernstfall: Der Online-Wahlkampf 2002', *Politik und Zeitgeschichte, Beilage: Das Parlament*, no. 49–50 (2002).

Hermens, F., *Demokratie oder Anarchie? Untersuchung über die Verhältniswahl*, 2nd edn (Cologne: Westdeutscher Verlag, 1968).

Herud, M., 'Die Empfehlungen zur Änderung des Parteiengesetzes', *Politische Vierteljahresschrift*, 42 (2001).

Hetterich, V., *Von Adenauer zu Schröder – Der Kampf um Stimmen* (Opladen: Leske & Budrich, 2000).

Hilmer, R., 'Bundestagswahl 2002: Eine zweite Chance für Rot-Grün', *Zeitschrift für Parlamentsfragen*, 34 (2003).

Hilmer, R. and N. Schleyer, 'Stimmensplitting bei der Bundestagswahl 1998: Strukturen, Trends und Motive', in J. van Deth, H. Rattinger and E. Roller, eds, *Die Republik auf dem Weg zur Normalität* (Opladen: Leske & Budrich, 2000).

Hirscher, G., *Kooperationsformen der Oppositionsparteien: Strategien und Positionen von SPD und Bündnis '90/Die Grünen und der Verhältnis zur PDS* (Munich: Hanns-Seidl Stiftung, 1997).

Hoffmann-Jaberg, B. and D. Roth, 'Die Nichtwähler: Normalität oder wachsende Distanz zu den Parteien?', in W. Bürklin and D. Roth, eds, *Das Superwahljahr* (Cologne: Bund-Verlag, 1994).

Holtz-Bacha, C., 'Massenmedien und Wahlen: Zum Stand der deutschen

Forschung – Befinde und Desiderata', in C. Holtz-Bacha and L. Kaid, eds, *Wahlen und Wahlkampf in den Medien* (Opladen: Westdeutscher Verlag, 1996).

Holtz-Bacha, C., *Wahlwerbung als politische Kultur* (Wiesbaden: Westdeutscher Verlag, 2000).

Holtz-Bacha, C. and L. Kaid, eds, *Wahlen und Wahlkampf in den Medien* (Opladen: Westdeutscher Verlag, 1996).

Ismayr, W., 'Das politische System Deutschlands', in W. Ismayr, ed., *Die politischen Systeme Westeuropas* (Opladen: Leske & Budrich, 1997).

Ismayr, W., ed., *Die politischen Systeme Westeuropas* (Opladen: Leske & Budrich, 1997).

Jesse, E., *Wahlrecht zwischen Kontinuität und Reform* (Düsseldorf: Droste Verlag, 1985).

Jesse, E., 'Die Bundestagswahlen 1972–1987 im Spiegel der repräsentativen Wahlstatistik', *Zeitschrift für Parlamentsfragen*, 18 (1987).

Jesse, E., 'Grundmandatsklausel und Überhangmandate: Zwei wahlrechtliche Eigentümlichkeiten in der Kritik', in M. Kaase and H-D Klingemann, eds, *Wahlen und Wähler: Analysen aus Anlass der Bundestagswahl 1994* (Wiesbaden: Westdeutscher Verlag, 1998).

Jesse, E., 'Reformvorschläge zur Änderung des Wahlrechts', *Aus Politik und Zeitgeschichte, Beilage: Das Parlament*, no. 52 (2003).

Jesse, E., 'Kontinuität und Wandel des Parteiensystems', *Das Parlament* (29 November 2004).

Just, D. and L. Romain, eds, *Auf der Suche nach dem mündigen Wähler* (Bonn: Bundeszentrale für politische Bildung, 1974).

Kaase, M., 'Determinanten des Wahlverhaltens bei der Bundestagswahl 1969', *Politische Vierteljahresschrift*, 11 (1970).

Kaase, M., 'Die Bundestagswahl 1972: Probleme und Analysen', *Politische Vierteljahresschrift*, 14 (1973).

Kaase, M. ed., 'Wahlsoziologie Heute: Analysen aus Anlass der Bundestagswahl 1976', special issue of *Politische Vierteljahresschrift*, 18 (1977a).

Kaase, M., 'Politische Meinungsforschung in der Bundesrepublik Deutschland', in M. Kaase, ed. 'Wahlsoziologie Heute: Analysen aus Anlass der Bundestagswahl 1976', special issue of *Politische Vierteljahresschrift*, 18 (1977b).

Kaase, M., 'Die Bundesrepublik Deutschland nach der Bundestagswahl 2002 – Überlegungen eines Wahlsoziologen', *Politische Vierteljahresschrift*, 44 (2003).

Kaase, M. and H.-D. Klingemann, eds, *Wahlen und politisches System* (Opladen: Westdeutscher Verlag, 1983).

Kaase, M. and H.-D Klingemann, eds, *Wahlen und Wähler: Analysen aus Anlass der Bundestagswahl 1994* (Wiesbaden: Westdeutscher Verlag, 1998).

Kaltefleiter, W., *Im Wechselspiel der Koalitionen. Eine Analyse der Bundestagswahl 1969* (Cologne, Berlin, Bonn, Munich: Carl Heymanns Verlag, 1970).

Kaltefleiter, W., 'Der Gewinner hat nicht gesiegt', *Aus Politik und Zeitgeschichte, Beilage: Das Parlament*, no. 50 (1976).

Kaltefleiter, W., 'Vorspiel zum Wechsel. Eine Analyse der Bundestagswahl 1976', *Verfassung und Verfassungswirklichkeit: Jahrbuch 1977* (Berlin: Duncker & Humblot, 1977).

Kepplinger, H., 'Die Kontrahenten in der Fernsehberichterstattung: Analyse einer Legende', in E. Noelle-Neumann, H. Kepplinger and W. Donsbach, *Kampa: Meinungsklima und Medienwirkung im Bundestagswahlkampf 1998* (Munich: Verlag Karl Alber Freiburg, 1999).

Klein, M and D. Ohr, 'Gerhard oder Helmut? "Unpolitische" Kandidateneigenschaften und ihre Einfluss auf die Wahlentscheidung bei der Bundestagswahl 1998', *Politische Vierteljahresschrift*, 41 (2001).

Kleinert, H., 'Schwarz-Grün erweitert Optionen', *Politische Meinung*, 49 (2004).

Klingemann, H.-D. and U. Pappi, 'Die Wählerbewegungen bei der Bundestagswahl am 28 September 1969', *Politische Vierteljahresschrift*, 11 (1970).

Knabl, G., 'Bei Anruf: Ihr Kandidat!', *Politik und Kommunikation* no.1 (2002).

Kohl, H., 'Regieren mit der FDP', in W. Mischnick, ed., *Verantwortung für die Freiheit: 40 Jahre FDP* (Stuttgart: DVA, 1988).

Kornelius, B., 'Politbarometer-Praxis: Die Trendwende vor der Bundestagswahl 2002', in A. Wüst, ed., *Politbarometer* (Opladen: Leske & Budrich, 2003).

Lange, E., *Wahlrecht und Innenpolitik* (Meisenheim: Anton Hain, 1975).

Lösche, P., 'Do electoral systems matter? Überlegungen am Beispiel Neuseelands', *Zeitschrift für Parlamentsfragen*, 35 (2004).

Luckemeyer, L., *Liberale in Hessen 1848–1980* (Frankfurt/Main: FDP Hessen, 1980).

Matz, C., 'Die Bedeutung des Internet für den Wahlkampf', in J. Schmid and H. Griese, eds, *Wahlkampf in Baden-Württemberg* (Opladen: Leske & Budrich, 2002).

Mayer, T. and R. Meier-Walser, eds, *Der Kampf um die politische Mitte: Politische Kultur und Parteiensystem seit 1998* (Munich: Olzog Verlag for the Hanns Seidel Stiftung, 2002).

Mende, E., *Von Wende zu Wende, 1962–1982* (Munich: Herbig, 1986).

Mischnick, W., ed., *Verantwortung für die Freiheit: 40 Jahre FDP* (Stuttgart: DVA, 1988).

Niedermayer, O., 'Parteimitgliedschaft im Jahre 2003', *Zeitschrift für Parlamentsfragen*, 35 (2004).

Noelle-Neumann, E., *Die Schweigespirale: Öffentliche Meinung – unsere sozial Haut* (Frankfurt/Main: Ullstein, 1982).

Noelle-Neumann, E., 'Öffentliche Meinung in der Bundestagswahl 1980', in M. Kaase and H.-D. Klingemann, eds, *Wahlen und politisches System* (Opladen: Westdeutscher Verlag, 1983).

Noelle-Neumann, E., H. Kepplinger and W. Donsbach, *Kampa: Meinungsklima und Medienwirkung im Bundestagswahlkampf 1998* (Munich: Verlag Karl Alber Freiburg, 1999).

Oppeland, T., 'Probleme der Volksparteien im Osten', in T. Mayer and R. Meier-Walser, eds, *Der Kampf um die politische Mitte: Politische Kultur und*

Parteiensystem seit 1998 (Munich: Olzog Verlag for the Hanns Seidel Stiftung, 2002).

Pappi, U. and S. Shikano, 'Personalisierung der Politik im Mehrparteiensystem am Beispiel deutscher Bundestagswahlen seit 1980', *Politische Vierteljahresschrift*, 42 (2001).

Pollack, D. and G. Pickel, 'Besonderheiten der politischen Kultur in Ostdeutschland als Erklärungsfaktoren der Bundestagswahl 1998 und die Rückwirkungen der Bundestagswahlen auf die politische Kultur Ostdeutschlands', in J. van Deth, H. Rattinger and E. Roller, eds, *Die Republik auf dem Weg zur Normalität* (Opladen: Leske & Budrich, 2000).

Pollmann, K., 'Wahlen und Wahlkämpfe in den Ländern der Bundesrepublik 1949–1960', in G. Ritter, ed., *Wahlen und Wahlkämpfe in Deutschland* (Düsseldorf: Droste Verlag, 1997).

Rabeneick, M., 'Der Bundestagswahlkampf 1976 der CDU', *Zeitschrift für Parlamentsfragen*, 10 (1979).

Radunski, P., *Wahlkämpfe* (Munich: Olzog Verlag, 1980).

Radunski, P., 'Wahlkampf in den achtziger Jahren', *Aus Politik und Zeitgeschichte, Beilage: Das Parlament*, no. 11 (1986).

Raschke, J. and R. Tils, 'CSU des Nordens: Profil und bundespolitische Perspektiven der Schill-Partei', *Blätter für deutsche und internationale Politik* (2002).

Rattinger, H., O. Gabriel and W. Jagodzinski, eds, *Wahlen und politische Einstellungen im vereinigten Deutschland* (Frankfurt/Main: Peter Lang, 1994).

Rauber, D., 'Überhangmandate – keine Überraschungen (mehr)', *Zeitschrift für Parlamentsfragen*, 34 (2003).

Recker, M.-L., 'Wahlen und Wahlkämpfe in der Bundesrepublik Deutschland 1949–1960', in G. Ritter, ed., *Wahlen und Wahlkämpfe in Deutschland* (Düsseldorf: Droste Verlag, 1997).

Reuner, F., 'Nachhaltigkeit durch Wahlrecht? Möglichkeiten und Grenzen eines "Wahlrecht von Geburt an"', *Zeitschrift für Parlamentsfragen*, 35 (2004).

Ritter, G., ed., *Wahlen und Wahlkämpfe in Deutschland* (Düsseldorf: Droste Verlag, 1997).

Roth, D and B. Kornelius, 'Europa und die Deutschen: Die untypische Wahl am 13. Juni 2004', *Aus Politik und Zeitgeschichte, Beilage: Das Parlament*, no. 17 (2004).

Schmid, J. and H. Griese, eds, *Wahlkampf in Baden-Württemberg* (Opladen: Leske & Budrich, 2002).

Schoen, H., 'Den Wechselwählern auf der Spur: Recall- und Paneldaten im Vergleich', in J. van Deth, H. Rattinger and E. Roller, eds, *Die Republik auf dem Weg zur Normalität* (Opladen: Leske & Budrich, 2000a).

Schoen, H., 'Eine oder zwei Stimmen – fundierte Debatte oder viel Lärm um nichts?, in J. van Deth, H. Rattinger and E. Roller, eds, *Die Republik auf dem Weg zur Normalität* (Opladen: Leske & Budrich, 2000b).

Schoen, H., 'Kandidatenorientierungen im Wahlkampf: Eine Analyse zu den Bundestagswahlkämpfen 1980–1998', *Politische Vierteljahresschrift*, 45 (2004).

Schoen, H. and J. Falter, 'Nichtwähler bei der Bundestagswahl 2002', *Politische Studien*, 54 (2003).

Sprickmann, D., 'Die "Erfindung" des Politbarometers', in A. Wüst, ed., *Politbarometer* (Opladen: Leske & Budrich, 2003).

Statistik von Baden, *Wahl zum Landtag von Baden-Württemberg am 24. März 1996* (Stuttgart: Statistisches Landesamt Baden-Württemberg, 1996).

Statistisches Bundesamt, 'Beim Bundeswahlleiter unterlegte Parteiunterlagen', file 76.3929 POL/Z PAR (Wiesbaden: Statistisches Bundesamt, 2002).

Sternberger, D., ed., *Wahlen und Wähler in Westdeutschland* (Villingen: Ring-Verlag, 1960).

Stöss, R. and G. Neugebauer, *Mit einem blauen Auge davon gekommen: Eine Analyse der Bundestagswahl 2002* (Berlin: Arbeitshefte aus dem Otto-Stammer-Zentrum, 2002).

Sturm, R. and H. Pehle, *Das neue deutsche Regierungssystem* (Opladen: Leske & Budrich, 2001).

Timm, A., *Die SPD-Strategie im Bundestagswahlkampf 1998* (Hamburg: Verlag Dr. Kovac, 1999).

Toman-Banke, M., 'Die Wahlslogans von 1949 bis 1994', *Aus Politik und Zeitgeschichte, Beilage: Das Parlament*, no. 51/52 (1994).

Toman-Banke, M., *Die Wahlslogans der Bundestagswahlen 1949–1994* (Wiesbaden: Deutscher Universitätsverlag, 1996).

van Deth, J., H. Rattinger and E. Roller, eds, *Die Republik auf dem Weg zur Normalität* (Opladen: Leske & Budrich, 2000).

Völker, M. and B. Völker, *Wahlenthaltung: Normalisierung oder Krisensymptom?* (Wiesbaden: Deutscher Universitätsverlag, 1998).

von Arnim, H., 'Entmündigen die Parteien das Volk?', *Aus Politik und Zeitgeschichte, Beilage: Das Parlament*, no. 21 (1990).

von Arnim, H., *Das System: Die Machenschaften der Macht* (Munich: Droemer, 2001).

von Webel, D., 'Der Wahlkampf der SPD', in E. Noelle-Neumann, H. Kepplinger and W. Donsbach, *Kampa: Meinungsklima und Medienwirkung im Bundestagswahlkampf 1998* (Munich: Verlag Karl Alber Freiburg, 1999).

Weixner, B., *Direkte Demokratie in den Bundesländern* (Opladen: Leske & Budrich, 2002).

Wessels, B., 'Kanzler- oder Politikwechsel? Bestimmungsgrunde des Wahlerfolgs der SPD bei der Bundestagswahl 1998', in J. van Deth, H. Rattinger and E. Roller, eds, *Die Republik auf dem Weg zur Normalität* (Opladen: Leske & Budrich, 2000).

Wilke, J. and C. Reinemann, *Kanzlerkandidaten in der Wahlkampfberichterstattung 1949–1998* (Cologne: Böhlau Verlag, 2000).

Wolf, W., *Der Wahlkampf: Theorie und Praxis* (Cologne: Verlag Wissenschaft und Politik, 1980).

Woyke, W., *Stichwort: Wahlen* (Bonn: Bundeszentrale für politische Bildung, 1994).

Wüst, A. ed., *Politbarometer* (Opladen: Leske & Budrich, 2003).

Zelle, C., 'Steigt die Zahl der Wechselwähler? Trends des Wahlverhaltens und der Parteiidentifikation', in H. Rattinger, O. Gabriel and W. Jagodzinski, eds, *Wahlen und politische Einstellungen im vereinigten Deutschland* (Frankfurt/ Main: Peter Lang, 1994).

Zolleis, U. and J. Schmid, 'Die Entwicklung zur Baden-Württemberg-Partei: Die CDU zwischen Heimat und High-Tech', in J. Schmid and H. Griese, eds, *Wahlkampf in Baden-Württemberg* (Opladen: Leske & Budrich, 2002).

Published in English

Andersen, R. and A. Zimdars., 'Class, education and extreme party support in Germany, 1991–98', *German Politics*, 12 (2003).

Anderson, C. and C. Zelle, eds, *Stability and Change in German Elections* (Westport, CT: Praeger, 1998).

Bogdanor, V., 'Conclusion: electoral systems and party systems', in V. Bogdanor and D. Butler, eds, *Democracy and Elections: Electoral Systems and their Political Consequences* (Cambridge: Cambridge University Press, 1983).

Bogdanor, V. and D. Butler, eds, *Democracy and Elections: Electoral Systems and their Political Consequences* (Cambridge: Cambridge University Press, 1983).

Brettschneider, F. and O. Gabriel, 'The nonpersonalization of voting behavior in Germany', in A. King, ed., *Leaders' Personalities and the Outcome of Democratic Elections* (Oxford: Oxford University Press, 2002).

Bulmer, S., C. Jeffery and W. Paterson, *Germany's European Diplomacy* (Manchester: Manchester University Press, 2000).

Curtice, J., 'Proportional representation in Scotland: public reaction and voter behaviour', *Representation*, 40 (2004).

Dinkel, R., 'The relationship between federal and state elections in West Germany', in M. Kaase and K. von Beyme, eds, *Elections and Parties* (London: Sage, 1978).

Eilders, C., K. Degenhardt, P. Herrmann and M. von der Lippe, 'Surfing the tide: an analysis of party and issue coverage in the national election campaign 2002', *German Politics*, 13 (2004).

Eilfort, M., 'Politikverdrossenheit and the non-voter', in G. Roberts, ed., *Superwahljahr: The German Elections in 1994* (London: Frank Cass, 1996).

Eith, U., 'Voting behavior in sub-national elections: local and state elections in three Länder, 1988–95', in C. Anderson and C. Zelle, eds, *Stability and Change in German Elections* (Westport, CT: Praeger, 1998).

Faas, T. and J. Maier, 'Chancellor-candidates in the 2002 televised debates', in C. Lees and T. Saalfeld, *The German General Election of 2002: The Battle of the Candidates*, special issue of *German Politics*, 13 (2004).

Gellner, W. and J. Robertson, *The Berlin Republic: German Unification and a Decade of Changes*, special issue of *German Politics*, 11 (2002).

Gibson, R., A. Römmele and S. Ward, 'German parties and internet campaigning in the 2002 federal election', *German Politics*, 12 (2003).

Gunlicks, A., 'The new German party finance law', *German Politics*, 4 (1995).

Harrison, L., 'The impact of German electoral systems upon extremist party representation: a comparative analysis', *Representation*, 37 (2000).

Helms, L., 'Turning indifference into a minor landslide: the 1999 European elections in Germany', *German Politics*, 8 (1999).

Helms, L, ed., *Institutions and Institutional Change in the Federal Republic of Germany* (Basingstoke: Macmillan, 2000).

Hogwood, P., 'The chancellor-candidates and the campaign', in C. Lees and T. Saalfeld, *The German General Election of 2002: The Battle of the Candidates*, special issue of *German Politics*, 13 (2004).

James, P., 'The Bavarian electoral system', *Electoral Studies*, 7 (1988).

Jeffery, C. and D. Hough, 'The electoral cycle and multi-level voting in Germany', in S. Padgett and T. Poguntke, eds, *Continuity and Change in German Politics: Beyond the Politics of Centrality?*, special issue of *German Politics*, 10 (2001).

Johnston, R. and C. Pattie, 'Campaigning and split-ticket voting in new electoral systems: the first MMP elections in New Zealand, Scotland and Wales', *Electoral Studies*, 21 (2002).

Jörs, I., 'East Germany: another party landscape', *German Politics*, 12 (2003).

Kaase, M. and K. von Beyme, eds, *Elections and Parties* (London: Sage, 1978).

Karp, J., J. Vowles, S. Banducci and T. Donovan, 'Strategic voting, party activity and candidate effects: testing explanations for split voting in New Zealand's new mixed system', *Electoral Studies*, 21 (2002).

King, A., ed., *Leaders' Personalities and the Outcome of Democratic Elections* (Oxford: Oxford University Press, 2002).

Kitschelt, H., 'Political–economic context and partisan strategies in the German federal elections 1990–2002', *West European Politics*, 26 (2003).

Kitzinger, U., *German Electoral Politics* (Oxford: Oxford University Press, 1960).

Kleinheinz, T., 'A new type of non-voter? Turnout decline in German elections, 1980–94', in C. Anderson and C. Zelle, eds, *Stability and Change in German Elections* (Westport, CT: Praeger, 1998).

Klingemann, H.-D. and B. Wessels, 'The political consequences of Germany's mixed-member system: personalization at the grass-roots?', in M. Shugart and M Wattenburg, eds, *Mixed-Member Electoral Systems* (Oxford: Oxford University Press, 2001).

Kommers, D., *The Constitutional Jurisprudence of the Federal Republic of Germany* (Durham, NC and London: Duke University Press, 1997).

Lees, C., *The Red–Green Coalition in Germany* (Manchester: Manchester University Press, 2000).

Lees, C. and T. Saalfeld, 'Introduction', in C. Lees and T. Saalfeld, *The German General Election of 2002: The Battle of the Candidates*, special issue of *German Politics*, 13 (2004a).

Lees, C. and T. Saalfeld, *The German General Election of 2002: The Battle of the Candidates*, special issue of *German Politics*, 13 (2004b).

Lessmann, S., *Budgetary Politics and Elections: An Investigation of Public*

Expenditures in West Germany (Berlin and New York: de Gruyter for the European University Institute, 1987).

McKay, J., 'The PDS tests the west: the Party of Democratic Socialism's campaign to become a pan-German Socialist party', *Journal of Communist Studies and Transition Politics*, 20 (2004a).

McKay, J., 'Women in German politics: still jobs for the boys?', *German Politics*, 13 (2004b).

Noelle-Neumann, E., 'The dual climate of opinion: the influence of television in the 1976 West German federal election', in M. Kaase and K. von Beyme, eds, *Elections and Parties* (London: Sage, 1978).

Parkes, K., *Writers and Politics in West Germany* (London: Croom Helm 1986).

Patzelt, W., 'Chancellor Schröder's approach to political and legislative leadership', in C. Lees and T. Saalfeld, *The German General Election of 2002: The Battle of the Candidates*, special issue of *German Politics*, 13 (2004).

Roberts, G., 'The "Second-Vote" Strategy of the West German Free Democratic Party', *European Journal of Political Research*, 16 (1988a).

Roberts, G., 'The German Federal Republic: the two-lane route to Bonn', in M. Gallagher and M. Marsh, *Candidate Selection in Comparative Perspective: The Secret Garden of Politics* (London: Sage, 1988b).

Roberts, G., 'Party system change in West Germany: Land–federal linkages', in P. Mair and G. Smith, *Understanding Party System Change in Western Europe* (London: Frank Cass, 1990).

Roberts, G., ed., *Superwahljahr: The German Elections in 1994* (London: Frank Cass, 1996).

Roberts, G., *Party Politics in the New Germany* (London: Pinter, 1997).

Roberts, G., 'The ever-shallower cleavage: religion and electoral politics in Germany', in D. Broughton and H.-M. ten Napel, *Religion and Mass Electoral Behaviour in Europe* (London: Routledge, 2000).

Roberts, G., 'Selection, voting and adjudication: the politics of legislative membership in the Federal Republic of Germany', *Government and Opposition*, 37 (2002).

Römmele, A., 'Communicating with their voters: the use of direct mailing by the SPD and the CDU', *German Politics*, 6 (1997).

Saalfeld, T., 'The German party system: continuity and change', in W. Gellner and J. Robertson, *The Berlin Republic: German Unification and a Decade of Changes*, special issue of *German Politics*, 11 (2002).

Shugart, M. and M Wattenburg, eds, *Mixed-Member Electoral Systems* (Oxford: Oxford University Press, 2001).

Trefs, M., 'Voter confusion in German federal elections: the Baden-Württemberg electoral system as a possible alternative', *German Politics*, 12 (2003).

Vowles, J., J. Karp and S. Banducci, 'Proportional representation on trial: elite vs. mass opinion on electoral system change in New Zealand', paper presented to American Political Science Association annual meetings, Washington. DC (2000).

Zelle, C., 'Social dealignment versus political frustration: contrasting explanations of the floating vote in Germany', *European Journal of Political Research*, 27 (1995).

Zelle, C., 'Candidates, issues and party choice in the federal election of 1994', in G. Roberts, ed., *Superwahljahr: The German Elections in 1994* (London: Frank Cass, 1996).

Index

Note: 'n.' after a page reference indicates the number of a note on that page.

5 per cent clause xi, 1, 4, 7–8, 12, 13,
  15, 18–19, 22, 23–4, 26n.3, 33,
  48, 49, 55, 60, 62, 63–4, 66,
  71n.5, 74, 76, 77, 81, 84, 91, 97,
  100, 101, 103, 105, 107, 111, 112,
  117n.8&9, 121, 123, 130, 133,
  137

abstentionism see turnout
Adenauer, Konrad 19, 29, 37, 42, 43,
  46, 70–1n.3, 75, 77, 78–9
Alliance '90 6, 22, 23, 90, 97n.6
  see also Green party
Anarchist Pogo Party 16
Arbeit für Bremen see Employment for
  Bremen party
Association of Free Citizens 5, 102,
  116n.3

Bad Godesberg Congress see Social
  Democratic Party
Barzel, Rainer 42, 83
Basic Law xi, 27–30, 37, 48n.1&2, 99,
  116n.3, 120, 123, 139
Bavarian Party 76
Biedenkopf, Kurt 25, 41
Brandt, Willy 39–40, 42, 43, 46,
  78–80, 83–4, 112, 122

Bundesrat xi, 82, 98–9, 109–10, 115,
  119, 125, 139
Bundestag xi, 23, 82–3, 117n.12,
  126–7n.1, 128, 132, 135, 139
  Standing Orders 29–30
  see also Bundestag elections;
    Members of the Bundestag
Bundestag elections 3–4, 124–5
  1949 20, 37, 73–5, 133
  1953 46, 66, 75–6, 122
  1957 37, 46, 47, 66, 71n.6, 76–8,
    110, 122
  1961 41, 67, 70–1n.3, 78–9
  1965 36, 39, 42, 68, 79–80,
    127n.2
  1969 39, 43, 46, 47, 60, 66, 68,
    71–2n.7, 80–2, 122
  1972 39, 40, 43, 46, 50, 66, 82–4,
    122, 127n.2
  1976 35, 46, 50, 84–5, 122, 127n.2
  1980 36, 40, 42, 43, 45, 46, 71n.6,
    85–6, 127n.2
  1983 45, 55, 66, 71n.6, 86–8
  1987 45, 66, 88–9
  1990 22–3, 25, 35, 36, 38, 45, 46,
    47, 50, 59, 89–90, 129, 130
  1994 23, 36, 43, 44, 54, 59, 62, 66,
    91–3, 114, 122, 129, 130

1998 26, 33, 35, 36, 41, 43, 44, 45,
    46, 47, 49n.5, 53, 55, 58–9, 61,
    62, 65, 66, 68, 93–4, 114, 122–3,
    129, 130
2002 14, 21, 26n.1, 32–3, 36, 38, 40,
    41, 43–5, 48, 49n.4, 51–2, 53–60,
    62–4, 65, 71n.5, 94–7, 113,
    122–3, 129, 130, 131
2005 140–2
Bundesversammlung xi, 98, 135
Bundeswahlleiter see Electoral
    Commissioner
Bund freier Bürger (BfB) see
    Association of Free Citizens

candidate selection 29, 31–5, 83
Centre Party (Z) 4, 16, 76
chancellor-candidate 35–6, 40, 41–4,
    75, 77, 78, 83, 84, 86, 87, 88, 89,
    93, 95, 112
Christian Democratic Union (CDU)
    4, 5, 6, 29, 33, 37, 39, 42, 43, 47,
    56, 58, 64, 65, 71n.6, 74, 75, 76,
    77, 78, 81, 83, 84, 85, 86, 87–8,
    90–2, 95, 96, 97n.2&5, 101,
    102–3, 106, 108, 109, 111, 112,
    114, 118, 130–2, 133, 140–2
    see also Christian Democrats
CDU–CSU see Christian Democrats
Christian Democrats (CDU–CSU) 4,
    5, 14, 19, 20, 21, 24, 26n.1, 36,
    38, 40, 41, 42, 44, 45, 46, 47, 48,
    55–7, 61, 62, 64, 66, 67, 71n.6,
    71–2n.7, 74–97, 109, 110–11,
    112, 118, 121–3, 135, 140–2
    electoral system preferences
        18–19
    religion and voting 56–7, 74–5, 82,
        85, 94, 97
    see also Christian Democratic
        Union; Christian Social Union
Christian Social Union (CSU) 4, 5, 6,
    29, 33–4, 43, 58, 64, 71n.6, 74,

75, 77, 78, 81, 82, 83, 85, 86, 87,
    91, 95, 99, 104, 107
    see also Christian Democrats
coalitions 3, 9, 21, 41, 47–8, 55, 64, 66,
    71n6, 71–2n.7, 73, 75–94, 96, 99,
    101, 107, 109–11, 112, 114,
    121–3, 124, 126, 127n.2, 130,
    131, 136
    see also 'grand coalition'; 'Jamaica'
        coalition; Magdeburg model
Communist Party (DKP) 16
Communist Party (KPD) 4, 16, 75, 76
constituencies
    pacts 66, 71–2n.7, 76, 133
    reapportionment 23, 24, 95, 131
Constitutional Court 7–8, 16, 21, 22,
    23–4, 28–30, 35, 44, 48n.1&2,
    116n.3, 126, 132, 140–2
    see also prohibition of parties
constructive vote of no confidence 42,
    83, 87, 122
cumulative voting 100, 116–17n.7

Democratic Awakening xi, 22
Deutsche Partei (DP) see German
    Party
Deutsche Sozial-Union (DSU) see
    German Social Union
Deutsche Volksunion (DVU) see
    German People's Union

election to Bundestag see Bundestag
    elections
election to Volkskammer 1990 see
    Volkskammer, election
electoral campaigns 2, 29, 73–97
    planning and organisation 35–40
    strategies 40–8
    treaties 30, 79
    see also Bundestag elections;
        chancellor-candidate; internet
        campaigning; Kampa project
Electoral Commissioner 16, 29

Electoral Law 15, 16, 18–20, 24,
    26n.1&2, 29, 76, 77, 128, 133,
    137
electoral pacts *see* constituencies,
    pacts
electoral politics 1, 2–4, 6–10, 118,
    126
electoral reforms 11, 12, 19, 20–1, 24,
    80, 105, 123, 125
electoral system 1, 12, 13–16,
    26n.1&2
    Bundestag election 1990 20, 22–3,
        89–90
    European Parliament 101
    evolution 16–21
    functions 121–4
    German constitution and 7–8,
        11–12, 15, 22, 23–4
    see also Constitutional Court
    German party system and 3–4,
        12–13
    Land elections 18, 24, 102–6
    local councils 100
    Volkskammer 1990 22
    see also Bundestag elections;
        Electoral Law; electoral reform;
        New Zealand electoral system;
        Second Empire electoral system;
        Weimar Republic
'*Elefantenrunde*' 38, 83
Employment for Bremen party 12,
    106
Erhard, Ludwig 20, 42, 74–5, 78–9,
    80, 97n.1
European Parliament elections 4, 29,
    91, 98, 101–2, 115–16n.2, 120

federal president *see* president,
    election of
Fischer, Joschka 39, 41, 62, 92, 94,
    95–6, 112
Fraktion *see* parliamentary party
    group

Free Democratic Party (FDP) 4, 5, 6, 7,
    10n.1, 12, 13, 14, 19, 20, 21, 25, 33,
    35–6, 38–40, 41, 44, 46, 48, 48n.2,
    57, 58, 64, 66, 67, 71n.6, 71–2n.7,
    75–97, 102, 107, 109, 110–11,
    121–3, 124, 130, 131, 135–6
    split-voting 3, 55, 61–2, 64–6, 71,
        82, 85, 94, 105, 131
Freie Demokratische Partei (FDP) *see*
    Free Democratic Party

Genscher, Hans-Dietrich 25, 41, 62,
    71n.6, 84, 86, 87–8, 90
German Association of Voters 20
German Party (DP) 19, 75, 76, 77, 133
German People's Union (DVU) 12,
    13, 59–60, 105, 106, 112
German Social Union (DSU) 5, 16, 90
'Grabenwahlsystem' *see* electoral
    reforms
'grand coalition' xii, 20, 46, 48, 60, 80,
    82, 92, 93, 109, 122, 123, 135,
    140–2
Grass, Günter 39, 79
Green party 5, 6, 12, 13, 14, 22, 23, 26,
    32, 33–4, 38, 41, 46, 48, 55–7, 66,
    86–97, 100, 101, 102, 106–7, 109,
    111, 112, 114, 115n.1, 121–3,
    124–5, 130–1, 135, 140–2
    split-voting 61–2, 64–5, 71n.5
    see also Alliance '90
Gysi, Gregor 41, 92, 95, 140

Hare-Niemeyer formula 106, 137–8
Heinemann, Gustav 20, 81, 136
Heuss, Theodor 75, 78, 135
d'Hondt method 105, 137–8

interest groups 3, 124
internet campaigning 38–9, 90, 95–6
invalid voting *see* voting behaviour

'Jamaica' coalition 151

Kampa project 35, 39, 46–7, 93–4, 95
Kiesinger, Kurt Georg 71–2n.7, 80–1,
    112
Kohl, Helmut 38, 42, 43, 44, 46, 47, 62,
    84, 87, 88, 89–92, 109, 111, 112
Köhler, Horst 135

Lafontaine, Oskar 36, 38, 42, 43,
    89–91, 94, 112
Land elections 9, 12–13, 52, 59, 60,
    73, 74, 82, 83, 85–6, 87, 88, 91,
    93, 97, 98–9, 108, 115, 118–19,
    120, 125
  Baden-Württemberg 56, 59, 103–4,
    116n.4&5
  Bavaria 34, 104–5, 116n.6,
    116–17n.7, 117n.8
  Bremen 105
  federal politics and 107, 108–15
  see also electoral system; Land
    elections
Left party 140–2
licensing of parties 4, 74
local council elections 99–101, 115n.1,
    120

Magdeburg model 91–2
Maier, Reinhold 75, 76, 110
mass media 8, 29, 30, 37–8, 44, 48n.2,
    68, 70, 72n.8, 75, 77, 78, 89, 124
Members of the Bundestag (MdBs)
    25–6, 26n.2, 34, 49n.4, 126, 140
  see also candidate selection
Mende, Erich 78–80, 81, 82, 83
Merkel, Angela 43, 64, 95, 118, 140–2
Möllemann, Jürgen 47, 96
Motorists Party 16

National Democratic Party (NPD) 3,
    13, 16, 21, 29, 59, 60, 80, 81, 106,
    112
New Zealand electoral system 11,
    26n.3, 53, 70n.2, 71n.4, 121

Ollenhauer, Erich 42, 75–7
opinion survey institutes 8, 67–8,
    69–70, 77, 113

panachage 100, 104, 116–17n.7
Parliamentary Council 12, 16, 17–18, 74
parliamentary party group xi–xii, 28,
    30, 33, 36, 97, 118
party finance 7, 28, 29, 37, 39, 120,
    127n.3
party foundations 28, 37
party identification 54, 58, 69
Party Law 15, 28–9, 48n.1, 120, 123
Party of Democratic Socialism (PDS)
    4, 6, 12, 13, 14, 15, 22, 23, 24, 30,
    33–4, 38, 41, 47, 48, 54, 58, 60,
    90–7, 100, 107, 110, 111, 113,
    115n.1, 124, 130, 132, 133, 135,
    140–2
  split-voting 26n.1, 62, 64, 65, 66,
    71n.5
Party of Non-Voters 16
party membership 6, 10n.1
party system 4–6, 27–31
  critiques of 30–1
Peace Union (FU) 77
permanent election campaign 119
president, election of 98, 135–6
prohibition of parties 8, 16, 29

Rau, Johannes 42, 88, 89, 112
referendums 99, 117n.9, 125–6
refugee party (GB-BHE) 110, 122
representative electoral statistics 69, 134
Republican party 12, 13, 22, 29, 59,
    102, 106, 112, 116n.4
reunification of Germany 4, 9, 22, 43,
    45, 128
right-wing extremism 3, 4–5, 52, 91,
    100, 113, 124
  see also German People's Union;
    National Democratic Party;
    Socialist Reich Party

Scharping, Rudolf 36, 42, 43, 44, 91–2, 112
Scheel, Walter 41, 47, 81–2, 83, 84
Schiller, Karl 43, 46
Schill party xii, 5, 12–13, 96, 106, 113
Schmidt, Helmut 42, 43, 84–5, 86–7, 122
Schröder, Gerhard (CDU) 81, 136
Schröder, Gerhard (SPD) 36, 38, 39, 40, 42, 43, 44, 47, 49n.6, 54, 59, 62, 70, 91, 93–6, 108, 112, 140–2
Schumacher, Kurt 29, 42, 74, 75
Second Empire electoral system 16–17
'second-order' elections 2, 98–9, 115
Social Democratic Party (SPD) 4, 6, 14, 29, 32, 33–4, 36–9, 41–3, 44, 45–8, 49n.6, 55–8, 61–6, 67, 71n.5&6, 74–97, 99, 101, 102–4, 106–7, 108–14, 116n.4&7, 121–3, 124, 126–7n.1, 127n.2, 130–2, 135–6, 140–2
   Bad Godesberg Congress 5, 7, 41, 78
   electoral system and 19, 20, 26n.1
   see also Kampa project
Socialist Reich Party (SRP) 16
'spiral of silence' thesis 68
split-voting 1, 3, 13, 14, 18, 19, 53, 60–6, 71n.4&5, 74, 82, 86, 94, 102, 105, 117n.8, 131
STATT party xii, 12–13, 106, 113
Stoiber, Edmund 36, 38, 42, 43, 44, 70, 95–6, 112
Stolpe, Manfred 41, 112
Strauss, Franz Josef 36, 40, 42, 43, 46, 71n.6, 80, 83, 86, 87, 97n.5
Ströbele, Christian 32, 63
'Superwahljahr' xiii, 93

surplus seats 9, 13, 14, 15, 21, 23–4, 26n.1&2, 47, 54, 65, 90, 92, 96, 102–5, 116n.4, 128–9, 130–2
surveys see opinion survey institutes

'three-seat' qualification 9, 13, 15, 20, 21, 23–4, 54, 77, 91, 92, 121, 133
turnout 13, 50–3, 70n.1, 75, 76, 78, 79, 80, 81, 84, 85, 86, 87, 89, 90, 93, 96, 100, 101, 106, 114, 124, 127n.3, 128–9

Überhangmandate see surplus seats
unification of Germany see reunification of Germany

Vogel, Hans-Jochen 42, 97, 112
Volkskammer xiii
   election 1990 22, 51
Volkspartei xiii, 39
voter initiative groups 39–40
voting behaviour 53–9, 68–70, 75, 76, 78, 81–2, 84, 85, 86, 88, 90, 93, 94, 96–7, 101, 102, 106, 108–9, 115–16n.2, 130, 134
   extremist voting 59–60
   invalid voting 53–4, 70–1n.3, 121
   'loaned' votes 55, 62, 87, 131
   see also split-voting; turnout

Weimar Republic 4, 27–8, 74, 75
   electoral system 12, 17
von Weizsäcker, Richard 30, 135
Wende xiii, 87, 88
Westerwelle, Guido 39, 44, 95

Zentrum see Centre party